Books should be returned on or before the
last date stamped below.

16. FEB. 1980

24. MAR. 1980

17. MAY 1980

18. JUN. 1980
19. JUL. 1980

26. JUL. 1980

13. AUG 1980

-1. OCT 1980

21. NOV 1980

14. NOV. 1981

-4. JUN 1972

-9. APR 1983
18. NOV. 1983

24. AUG 1984

2 3 FEB 1985

1 9 APR 1986

2 7 MAY 1987

JUL 87 7 5

- JAN 89 6 3

- JUN 89 3 8

OLDUVAI GORGE:
MY SEARCH FOR EARLY MAN

MARY D. LEAKEY

———————◆———————

OLDUVAI GORGE:
My Search
for Early Man

COLLINS
ST JAMES'S PLACE, LONDON

William Collins Sons & Co Ltd
London · Glasgow · Sydney · Auckland
Toronto · Johannesburg

First published 1979
© Mary D. Leakey 1979
ISBN 0 00 211613 8
Set in Imprint
Made and Printed in Great Britain by
William Collins Sons & Co Ltd Glasgow

CONTENTS

LIST OF MAPS AND PLANS

LIST OF PLATES

ACKNOWLEDGEMENTS

I would like to express my appreciation to the United Republic of Tanzania for continued permission to work at Olduvai Gorge and, personally, to Mr A. A. Mturi, Director of Antiquities, for his most helpful co-operation. The Conservator of Ngorongoro, Mr A. N. J. Mgina, has been of unfailing help to me in many different ways. He has my most sincere thanks.

Not only I, but all who are interested in the study of early man, must be immeasurably grateful to the National Geographic Society of Washington, DC for their continued support over the last eighteen years.

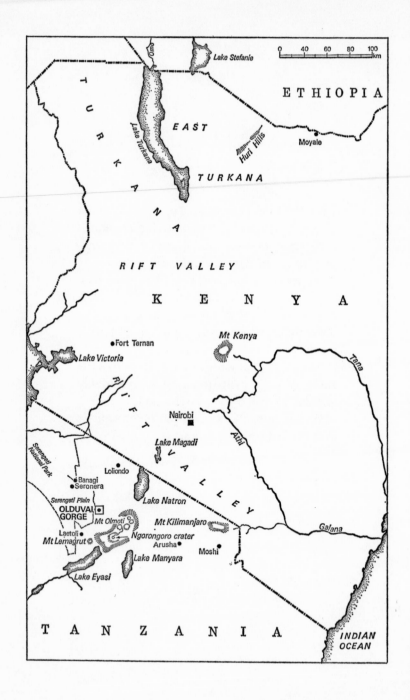

CHAPTER ONE
Introduction to Olduvai

OLDUVAI GORGE is a unique geological feature in the Serengeti plains, and has been likened to a small-scale Grand Canyon. It is fifty kilometres long and in places as much as ninety metres deep, cutting down almost vertically through ancient lake beds where the remains of early man and his tools are found. The vegetation in the vicinity of the gorge is typical of the hot, dry part of Africa: short grass on the open plains with scattered umbrella thorn trees and scrub. Within the gorge itself there is abundant wild sisal or Sansevieria, from which the Masai name of Olduvai is derived. It is pronounced Ol-doo-vye, with a short O, as in orange, and means 'the place of the wild sisal'. 'Wait-a-bit' thorn bushes (*Acacia mellifera*) are common in the gorge. They generally come into flower in June, before the leaves appear, when the bushes become covered with small, fluffy white or cream-coloured flowers that give off an incredibly sweet scent, reminiscent of orange blossom. For a short while the gorge is transformed and resembles a fruit orchard in full bloom. The vernacular name of these thorns is very apt since the branches bear small, sharply backward-curved thorns which hook stubbornly into one's clothing. Umbrella thorns (*Acacia tortilis*) are mostly found in valleys and along dry river courses. Their flowering is less spectacular and generally takes place at the approach of rain, when there is increased humidity in the atmosphere, but before the rain has actually fallen.

The climate is hot and dry for most of the year, with shade temperatures around thirty degrees centigrade. Owing to the wind that blows almost constantly from the east, it is seldom unpleasantly hot. Systematic records of the rainfall have only been kept at Olduvai since 1967. During that time the average has been fifty-seven centimetres per year, but there are years when it is much drier.

At the head of the gorge there are two adjacent lakes, Llgarja (or Ndutu) and Masek; the latter overflows into the river during exceptionally wet years. In its upper reaches the Olduvai River is a shallow water course, running through a wide valley; but about twenty-five kilometres from the lakes, where it cuts down into the Pleistocene sediments, the valley changes abruptly into a steep-sided gorge. A subsidiary branch, known as the side gorge, drains from Lemagrut Mountain and joins the main gorge about eight kilometres from the mouth, which is in the fault trough of the Olbalbal Depression. Although neither so deep nor so spectacular as the main gorge, this branch follows the shore line of the prehistoric lake and is particularly rich in fossils and living sites of early man.

Olduvai Gorge was first made known to the scientific world in 1911, when Tanzania, or German East Africa, as it was then called, was under German rule. The gorge was discovered accidentally by Professor Kattwinkle, a German entomologist who was hunting butterflies on the Serengeti. He collected some fossil bones, including teeth of the three-toed horse, and took them back with him to Berlin. There they aroused great interest, to the extent that the Kaiser himself gave his personal support to an expedition to Olduvai.

This first expedition, under the leadership of Professor Hans Reck, a geologist, came out in 1913. It amassed a large number of fossils and also discovered a human skeleton which Professor Reck considered to be contemporary with the fossil fauna and to be of Middle Pleistocene age. Part of this skeleton has recently been dated by radio carbon and is about 17,000 BP (before the present). The results of the 1913 expedition made such an impact on German scientific circles that the following year no fewer than four expeditions planned to set forth for Olduvai from Germany, but owing to the outbreak of the First World War none of them reached their destination. At the close of the war Tanzania became a British Mandated Territory.

My husband Louis first came to Olduvai in 1931, accompanied by Professor Reck. By present-day standards the expedition had to endure extreme difficulties. The journey from Nairobi took seven days, travelling via Loliondo, instead of eight and a half hours, as today, via Arusha. There was no road open to vehicular traffic over Ngorongoro and stores had to be brought from Nairobi at considerable expense. Water had to be obtained from a small spring on the slopes of Olmoti, where it was necessary to wait twenty minutes in order to fill an eighteen-litre can. It then had to be carried on foot for several kilometres to the nearest point to which the lorry could be driven.

Before coming out on the 1931 expedition Louis had examined the collection of fauna from Olduvai in Berlin, and was convinced that stone tools would be found in the same deposits. He based his belief on the discovery of handaxes at Kariandusi in Kenya, in deposits that were then thought to belong to the Kamasian Pluvial, which he considered to be of about the same age as the Olduvai beds. Professor Reck was equally convinced that no tools would be found, a view that is hard to credit nowadays, when

Olduvai has provided the most complete record in the world of early man and his tools. In fact, Louis and an African member of his staff found a number of handaxes within a hundred metres of the 1931 camp site a few hours after they arrived.

My first visit to Olduvai was in 1935, when I was twenty-two years old. I had been on a visit with my mother to prehistoric sites in South Africa and Rhodesia. Leaving her to return to England by boat from Cape Town, I flew up to join Louis at Moshi, a small town lying at the foot of Kilimanjaro. I arrived in April, at the height of the rainy season. Even the main road south from Arusha was merely a dirt track in those days and during the rains it sometimes became impassable in parts. We made the trip to Olduvai in an old wooden 'box body' Rugby car. After leaving the main road we climbed up 600 metres to the rim of the extinct crater of Ngorongoro, now visited annually by many thousands of tourists on account of the scenic beauty of the area and the vast concentrations of game on the crater floor. The road to Ngorongoro was then described as a 'dry weather track'. During the rainy season it became a quagmire and was so bad that it took us three days to get the car eighteen kilometres to the top, where the present Crater Lodge is situated. Stores had been sent on ahead by lorry directly to Olduvai, so that during the three days spent pushing the car and digging it out of the mud the only food we had was several bunches of bananas and a few tins of sardines. We had no stove and all kindling was so saturated by the rain that we could not even make tea.

The view coming down the west flank of Ngorongoro Crater on to the Serengeti plains impressed me greatly and has never, to the present day, ceased to delight me. Rising above the plain to the south and east are the great volcanoes – Lemagrut, Ngorongoro and Olmoti – from which the

Serengeti plain stretches away into the distance to the west.

In 1935 we were able to drive as far as the camp site, at the confluence of the main and side gorges, but our vehicles were unsuitable for driving across country – nor did we have enough petrol for anything except essential transport of water and supplies. All our exploration of the gorge had to be done on foot. We would start out very early in the morning, taking water bottles, and stay out until three or four in the afternoon. If we found fossils, we had to carry them back to camp ourselves.

I remember when we found the skull of an extinct hippopotamus – *H. gorgops* – about three kilometres from camp up the side gorge. Before it could be moved it had to be enclosed in a plaster of Paris jacket. This meant taking water, plaster, hessian, mixing bowl, etc., to the site. Nowadays, with very much better preservatives that harden the bones throughout, it is seldom necessary to plaster a fossil. But in the 1930s and 1940s we only had shellac as a preservative and this was far from satisfactory. The process of removing a large fossil was lengthy. The top of the fossil and the sides would first be carefully cleared of soil, then covered with wet toilet paper, pushed well into the crevices. Strips of previously wetted hessian dipped into plaster of Paris were then placed over the top and sides, overlapping one another. When the plaster had set the fossil was undercut and turned over, and the underside received similar treatment. In the case of very heavy specimens such as the hippo skull, reinforcing iron bars or strong pieces of timber were plastered on before removal. To transport this skull Louis made a stretcher from poles pushed through sacks, which he and three men managed to carry the three kilometres back to camp.

In those days it was possible to shoot for meat on the Serengeti and Louis occasionally shot a Grant's or Thomson's gazelle. Other food, however, eventually became nearly exhausted, and the lorry was dispatched to Nairobi for fresh supplies. It failed to return on schedule; indeed, it was delayed for over a week. During that time our diet was reduced to boiled rice and apricot jam, which finally became quite nauseating. In those days, too, Louis and I were both heavy smokers, and when our cigarettes were finished we collected all the old stubs from round the camp and re-rolled them in toilet paper, which was then of a substantial variety known as Bronco.

Eventually Louis and I set out in search of the lorry. Not far from Loliondo, Louis capsized the car into an erosion gully alongside the road. The gully was as deep as the car was wide and it lay with the offside level with the road, fitting neatly into the ditch. Without assistance or suitable tools it seemed a hopeless task to try to get it out, but we set to work with our small, specially-made excavating picks and used two enamel soup plates as shovels. After a long time we reached the point where the car could be righted on to its four wheels again. Ironically, our lorry turned up just then and our men soon pushed us back on to the road. During the long hours when we had been digging, groups of young Masai warriors had come to watch us with great amusement; they did not offer to help.

On this visit to Olduvai we had no means of transporting water from any distance and we were forced to use the water in the gorge. When it is still fresh, shortly after the rain has fallen, the water in the side gorge is quite palatable, although very cloudy, with fine sediment in suspension. But as time goes on and it remains standing in pools that are used by the game it becomes most unpleasant, since many animals, including rhinos, often urinate at waterholes. An attempt to filter this water through charcoal met with no success, so that our soup, tea or coffee all tasted of rhino urine, which we never quite got used to. One day a shower of rain fell in camp, and we eagerly collected the water from the tents in every possible container. It looked so clean and pure that we drank it immediately, forgetting that the tent canvas had been impregnated with poison against termites and other insects. Within minutes, each one of us was vomiting violently. Fortunately we all recovered and there were no serious after-effects.

As well as Sam Howard, a personal friend of Louis's, we had with us in 1935 two young men who had just finished at Cambridge and were waiting to enter the Colonial Service: Peter Bell, who later became District Commissioner in Tanzania, collected birds for the British Museum; and Stanhope White, who made a plane table map of part of the gorge and afterwards entered the Nigerian Colonial Service. There was also a young geologist, P. E. Kent, who, many years later, was knighted for his work on petroleum.

The three months we spent at Olduvai that year were mainly devoted to work in the side gorge, which had received little attention until then. A number of sites rich in both fossils and stone tools were recorded for the first time and named after members of the expedition.

Our early work at Olduvai was carried out on a shoe-string. From time to time Louis was able to raise enough funds for us to visit the gorge for a few weeks, when we did some hurried digging and fossil-hunting. On our brief visits in 1941, 1953, 1955 and 1957 we continued to find stone tools and well-preserved fossilized bones of animals which convinced us that the remains of Olduvai's early hominid inhabitants must eventually come to light.

At last, during the 1959 season, I was fortunate enough to discover the skull of 'Zinjanthropus' or Australopithecus boisei. Since the skull was associated with stone tools we believed for a while that we had found one of the makers of the early stone industry from Olduvai, known as the

Oldowan. The subsequent discovery of a second type of early hominid, *Homo habilis*, with a relatively larger brain capacity, changed this view. '*Zinjanthropus*' in fact represents an extinct side-line of hominid evolution not in the direct ancestry of man and probably a tool-user rather than a tool-maker.

From 1959 on we were assured of financial support for the Olduvai excavations, and work has continued systematically ever since.

1962 was the first year that the geologist Dr Richard L. Hay came to Olduvai. From then until 1974 he visited the gorge during almost every summer vacation. Before he unravelled the complex stratigraphy of Olduvai the relationship of many of the sites remained uncertain. For example, sites in the side gorge could not be correlated with those in the main gorge. The framework of the stratigraphic sequence of stone industries in Beds I and II that was published in Volume 3 of the Olduvai monographs* is based entirely on his work. It is probably true to say that the close collaboration between geological and archaeological studies can seldom have produced such worthwhile results as at Olduvai.

Since the discovery of the skull of '*Zinjanthropus*', Olduvai has become almost synonymous in the public mind with research into the prehistory of man. Yet it is important to realize that Olduvai is not the whole story. Research in other parts of the world preceded ours at Olduvai and important research is continuing in other localities at the present time. In 1978, for example, evidence relating to early man and the contemporary fauna was found in the form of fossilized footprints at Laetoli, a Pliocene site forty-five kilometres south of Olduvai.

Moreover, disciplines other than archaeology have played a

* Cambridge University Press, 1971.

vital role in this work. Our aim at Olduvai, which we share with all prehistoric archaeologists and palaeo-anthropologists, is to try to determine when and by what steps our ancestors became human and evolved into *Homo sapiens*. Essentially, the remains of early man are preserved in sedimentary rocks. The processes by which sedimentary rocks are formed generally permit only tough, resistant objects to be preserved. As a result, our record of early man consists of stone tools and resistant bones, teeth and mandibles, with occasional skulls. From these we are able to deduce a considerable amount about his physical characteristics and capabilities, his way of life and his contemporary environment.

CHAPTER TWO
The Camp

I HAD NO WAY of knowing, when I first visited Olduvai, what an important role it was to play in my life and that I would eventually come to live there in a permanent camp, as I do nowadays.

My living conditions are simple and to many would seem primitive and uncomfortable; but lack of amenities is more than made up for by the delight of living out in the wilds, in the most beautiful scenery, surrounded by animals in their natural habitat. It is one of my pleasures, too, that there is no radio, no telephone and no newspapers. My communication with the outside world is by means of a radio telephone, by which I can make outward calls, but nobody can call me without previous arrangement. But the camp is by no means isolated: there is a constant stream of overseas scientists visiting Olduvai to pursue their studies in one field or another, contributing to the many aspects of the study of early man.

Living quarters at Olduvai have been enlarged and improved over the course of years. In 1935 and during our subsequent brief visits we lived in small, low tents. They were uncomfortably hot, and always presented difficulties owing to the strong winds and to the fact that tent pegs could not be driven through the limestone that covers the plains under the loose surface soil.

In 1960, when funds had become available for a prolonged field season, we put up an oblong grass house on the north side of the main gorge to serve as work-room and living quarters. A refrigerator was also installed, which proved to be an invaluable asset to the camp. Tents were still used for sleeping, although my dogs and I slept in a truck that had been converted into a caravan. Sleeping quarters that could be securely fastened at night were essential in order to safeguard the dogs against leopards, who are capable of tearing through a tent.

This camp had fallen into disrepair by 1968 and my son Richard arranged for the men to build a new camp for me opposite the old site, but on the west side of the gorge and off the main tourist route. This was more ambitious than the previous camp and a great deal more comfortable. A larger grass house was built, giving more space for working and dining. It was open to the south, with a magnificent view of Lemagrut Mountain. I myself was allocated a round tin hut known as a 'uniport' that is made in sections for easy transport and then assembled on the spot. This has a cement floor and is roofed over with a grass thatch to keep it cool. After the small grass hut with an earth floor that I had lived in at the first camp this seemed the height of luxury, especially since it did not harbour so many spiders. My hut also has glazed windows so that it is possible to work on plans and drawings even during a strong wind. Indeed, the advantages of buildings that are wind and weather proof have proved so great that I have built similar huts for the African staff and for visitors to the camp.

In 1973 we were most thankful to be housed safely in lion-proof dwellings, since a pride of eight starving young lions prowled round the camp for several nights. They had no adults with them to teach them how to hunt or to hunt for them (the parents had either abandoned them or been killed by Masai warriors). The young lions were so incapable of hunting wild prey that while they were at Olduvai they lived exclusively on Masai cows, donkeys, goats and dogs. In fact, they even ate one of the Head Guide's cross-bred Dalmatian dogs. One night they also made an attempt to get at my dogs who slept in the hut with me. One of the lions jumped against my window and shattered the glass, but there was an iron grille on the inside that prevented him from getting in. For quite a while afterwards I had a recurrent nightmare in which I saw the head of a lion appear at an open window that I was unable to shut since I was holding the four dogs to restrain them from attacking the lion.

These young lions eventually became so desperately hungry that they killed and ate a Masai child that was sleeping with the goats in one of the villages. Then one night they left Olduvai and migrated to Lake Ndutu, at the head of the gorge. By the time they arrived there they were so weak with hunger that they could barely lift their heads. Fortunately George Dove, who owned the Ndutu Lodge, was able to look after them for several months until they regained their strength and were able to fend for themselves.

In 1974 my camp was further enlarged and improved. Thanks to the generosity of Gordon Hanes of Winston Salem, North Carolina (who financed it) and the kindness of George Dove (who supervised the building) a fine breeze-block living-room, study and pantry were built immediately behind the grass hut that had served as dining-, living- and work-room since 1968. The new building not only made life very much more comfortable, but also provided a means of collecting rain water. The thatched roofs of the 1960s were, regretfully, replaced by corrugated iron, from which clean water is drained into a number of large tanks.

The living-room is open to the south-east and like the former grass hut has a magnificent view of Lemagrut Mountain.

The only people who live at Olduvai besides ourselves are the Masai. All travellers in East Africa are familiar with the Masai *morani* (warriors) with their flowing red robes, braided hair, ear-rings and business-like spears. The Masai are a nomadic people who have survived and maintained their social structure and culture in a harsh, semi-arid environment. Their diet is mainly milk mixed with blood, which is drawn from their cattle and donkeys at regular intervals. At Olduvai there are numbers of Masai *manyattas* or homesteads – low, loaf-shaped huts made from bent branches plastered with cow dung and surrounded by thorn fences.

The Masai make use of the grazing as long as water lasts in the gorge; but during the game migration, which coincides with the wildebeest calving, they either move up on to the slopes of the mountains or restrict their cattle to thorn-fenced enclosures along the rim of the gorge, with scarecrows outside in order to keep off the wildebeest. This is because the Masai believe that wildebeest calves carry malignant catarrh, a disease to which the calves are mostly immune, but to which cattle have no resistance. Every year the Masai set alight the slopes of the mountains that lie to the south and east of Olduvai, supposedly to encourage the growth of new grass at the beginning of the rains and also to reduce the numbers of ticks; but each year the fires encroach further and further into the remaining forested areas, and it is evident that if the present rate of destruction continues the mountains will become denuded of forest and unable to conserve rain water.

In 1935 the massacre of lions by tourists at Banagi in what is now the Seronera National Park brought about the prohibition of shooting lions in the Seronera area and in part of Ngorongoro. Two years later a complete ban came into force on shooting all the big carnivores, as well as rhinoceros, giraffe and rarer animals. In 1940, both the Serengeti and Ngorongoro were declared a National Park. This action was taken summarily, without the knowledge or consent of the Masai, who suddenly found themselves inhibited as to travel and the number of stock they could own within the Park. Cultivation was also banned. Although this did not affect the true-blooded pastoralist Masai, it resulted in the eviction of the squatters belonging to the Warusha and Wambulu tribes who farmed within the Park boundaries. While their evacuation of both Ngorongoro and Embagai Craters was urgently necessary, since cultivation was taking place on an alarming scale, their removal from other areas possibly caused unnecessary hardship.

Resentment among the Masai against the Park's ordinance, in which human interests take second place to the welfare of the game, built up over the years. Such pressure was brought to bear on the authorities that it was suggested, in order to mollify the Masai, that the Serengeti Park including Ngorongoro should be broken up into a series of small parks, game reserves, controlled areas, etc. This proposal rightly led to an unprecedented outcry by wildlife bodies and conservationists in East Africa, England and the United States. As a result a Committee of Enquiry was set up in Arusha. Louis was a member, together with legal experts, representatives of the leading wildlife bodies and a host of others concerned with ecology, veterinary science, water engineering, etc. After much deliberation and examination of reports the committee created the present Conservation Area, which covers Ngorongoro and the eastern Serengeti, including Olduvai Gorge – the only part of Olduvai to remain within the Park being Lake Ndutu at the head of the gorge. In return for the establishment of the Conservation Area, in which human rights were recognized on an equal basis to those of the wildlife, the Masai ceded certain areas of the western Serengeti to the Park.

Before the dispensary at Ngorongoro was adequately staffed and supplied with drugs, one of our tasks at Olduvai was treating the sick Masai. There were often as many as fifteen in a day, sometimes more. Most of them were genuine cases, but a number of elderly women used to turn up regularly, day after day, with one excuse or another, most probably for the pleasure of exchanging gossip with their cronies from neighbouring homesteads.

The stoicism shown by the Masai in the face of physical pain is beyond belief. Occasionally, when *morani* were gored by rhinos or mauled by lions, we would be asked to fetch them from their homes and take them to hospital. Once two young *morani* – mere teenage boys – were brought into camp after they had fought a lion that had made off with one of their cows. Both had been severely mauled and one had a triangular flap of flesh, about twenty centimetres long, torn from his back, so that the bone of his shoulder blade was showing. His friend had pinned it roughly back into place with thorns. He remained fully conscious and capable of sitting upright in the Land-Rover during the forty-kilometre journey to hospital.

Many babies and small children were brought in with appalling burns: it seemed that Masai mothers took few precautions to safeguard their children from falling into the fire. In some cases wet cow dung had been plastered over the burns. When this had been left undisturbed the wounds were usually clean and fresh skin had begun to form. More often, the burns had been wrapped round with filthy rags and had become infected.

Nearly all the babies and children, as well as many of the adults, suffer from an eye disease called trachoma, which is fly-borne. It is hardly surprising that it is so common, since the Masai live in a perpetual swarm of flies, to which they appear to be wholly oblivious, allowing them to crawl over their faces and eyes without making any attempt to brush them away. Trachoma can be cured within two weeks by daily application of antibiotic ointment, but we found it was seldom possible to effect a cure. Within a few days of starting the course, when improvement became visible, the children were taken back to their villages and we could not complete the treatment. Suppurating ears and running sores were also common among the children. One small boy whom we had treated for an ulcer on his leg left for home still wearing a bandage. When he returned to our camp about four months later he still wore the same bandage, which he informed us proudly had never been removed.

As far as we are concerned the most serious problem presented by the Masai who live near the gorge is the damage that their herds of cattle do by trampling over fossils. As a result of the destruction of two hominid skulls in this way, a meeting was called between the Conservator of Ngorongoro, the local government officials, the Masai elders and ourselves, in order to come to an agreement for keeping the cattle off the fossil beds. After a day-long discussion the elders agreed that they would instruct the herd boys to keep the cattle out of any areas which we enclosed with thorn fences. In return, Louis undertook to construct two dams to conserve water for the Masai. The National Geographic Society once more came to our aid with a special grant for this purpose and Louis was able to build two dams, one across the main gorge and the second across the side gorge. Unfortunately by 1970 they had both become full of silt and no longer held water.

In spite of genuine co-operation from the Masai elders in trying to keep the cattle out of the fenced areas, the herd boys do not always obey their instructions and cattle still do considerable damage. The Ngorongoro Conservation Authority, with generous financial aid from Mr Gordon Hanes, has now installed a pipe line to bring water down from Olmoti Mountain to drinking troughs in the Olbalbal Depression. In return, the Masai have moved their *manyattas* away from the gorge to areas within reach of the new water supply.

Every year, vast herds of wildebeest and zebra migrate through the Olduvai area during January and February, when there is ample grazing, following the rains. The wildebeest calves are born at this time and many get separated from their mothers as the herds stampede across the gorge. Many of them end up as the victims of hyaenas or cheetah. Unlike zebra, who move in an orderly fashion, wildebeest tend to panic when confronted with an unusual situation, such as finding themselves in a confined space within the gorge. They get so disturbed that they seem to become oblivious to people; and I have been told by the wildlife photographers Alan and Joan Root that they will not deviate from their course even if slapped on the rump as they stream past.

Although there is an overall pattern of movement that the plains animals follow year after year, their local movements seem to depend largely on the rainfall in different areas. During years when the rains last for an appreciable time, the herds come and go over a period of several weeks.

With the herbivorous plains game come the predators – lion, cheetah, wild dogs and packs of hunting hyaenas. The animals permanently resident at Olduvai include rhino, giraffe, dik dik (a small, dry-country antelope), klipspringers (an antelope that inhabits rocky terrain), spring hares, bat-eared foxes, hyaenas, jackals, mongooses, porcupines, a few cheetah and a few leopards. Herds of Grant's and Thomson's gazelles come with the zebra and wildebeest during the migration and some remain in the area for part of the dry season but eventually move elsewhere.

The bird life at Olduvai is remarkably abundant, considering the dryness of the locality. In order to make a comparison with the large numbers of fossil birds that have been found at different sites in the gorge I have attempted to list the varieties now living in the area. Even though there are some birds that I have been incapable of identifying, the list has reached a figure of over seventy. Among these it is interesting to note several that are recorded among the fossils, such as hoopoes and mousebirds, as well as Fischers love birds, whose present-day distribution is centred in northern Tanzania. The aquatic birds, such as pelicans, flamingoes and cormorants, which were common in prehistoric times when there was a permanent lake, do not, of course, occur today. But one or more pairs of Egyptian geese nest and rear their young each year in the water left standing in the river bed after the rains. Migrants also pass through from time to time, such as storks, swallows, and various other European birds, including the rock thrush, the European roller, the wheatear, etc. A few storks ringed in Germany have also been found on the Serengeti.

We have always shared our camp at Olduvai with a variety of birds and beasts, wild and tame. The Dalmatians are a permanent feature. In 1963 and 1964 we also had in camp a small fox terrier bitch, who perpetually caused dog fights, and a pet monkey called Simon. He was a young Sykes monkey that my son Richard had found being hawked round in Nairobi. Probably no pet of mine has ever been so unpopular as Simon. His capacity for exasperating and infuriating everyone was beyond measure, but he was unusually good-tempered and friendly, so that he generally had free run of the camp. I never discovered, to the day I finally put him in the Nairobi animal orphanage, whether mischief-making was his idea of fun, or whether it was due to stupidity.

He was fascinated by cosmetics, and any female visitor was liable to have her bags raided and her toilet articles scattered round the camp. The specimens from the excavations fortunately did not attract his attention to quite the same extent, but he found the coloured pencils used by Richard Hay for geological sections and maps quite irresistible. He had marked likes and dislikes, too, among visitors to the camp. Perhaps his favourite was George Dove. George possessed – and still does – the most magnificent pair of moustaches that I have ever seen, each several inches long and waxed to a delicate, tapering point. Simon was bewitched by them and would sit on George's shoulder gently fingering and sniffing his moustaches.

When we returned to our house near Nairobi we made a large wire enclosure for Simon, but he invariably found ways of getting out. His final downfall came one day when he let himself out of his cage on an afternoon when nobody was in the house. Among other things he opened the drinks cupboard and either accidentally or intentionally broke three bottles that had contained whisky, sherry and Drambuie. He was later found by our house servant sprawled face downwards in the pool of mixed liquor, totally unconscious: even treatment under the cold tap did not arouse him for several hours. After this episode he was taken to the animal orphanage, where he settled down quite happily with a little lady monkey.

At that time we also had a tame wildebeest calf which we had found abandoned on the plains during the calving season and reared on a bottle. Louis named him Oliver, on account of his insatiable appetite. When we first caught him he was very wild and had to be kept on a rope, but within twenty-four hours he came to regard me as his mother and followed me everywhere.

Young wildebeest calves are a most attractive colour: pale fawn at birth, turning to a rich golden yellow after a few weeks, with black masks, ears and tips to their tails. They also have exceedingly long black eye-lashes and eye-brows, that curl down over their eyes and partially hide them. Their only defence is speed; and when they are first born their legs are very long in proportion to their bodies. Even a newborn calf can keep up with the herd. But many get separated from their mothers during the annual migration, when the herd is either stampeded by lions, or panics for one reason or another. It is a very sad sight to see the orphans trailing along at the rear of the herds – sooner or later to weaken and die or be eaten by predators.

Oliver was one of the most entertaining and lovable pets I have ever had. He was extremely mischievous, but unlike Simon he was sufficiently intelligent to realize when one of his pranks had gone far enough and we were beginning to get annoyed. He habitually accompanied the dogs on their walks and eventually must have come to regard himself as part-canine as well as part-human; for one day, when he and I were out walking without the dogs, he chased a hare. When he caught up with it he was nonplussed as to what his next move should be and stood gazing at it in puzzlement. He also loved to tease people and would chase visitors round the camp, particularly children and young people, whom he clearly expected to join in the game. Until he reached the age of about six months he would desist from his games if I scolded him and whacked the ground with a stick, and would respond by going down on his knees in front of me. While this appeared to human eyes to be a gesture of apology, I always believed it may have had a very different meaning in wildebeest behaviour.

One of the pastimes that he found most entertaining was to charge into the tents when any of the girls were bathing in the evenings. We would see Oliver standing outside their tent with his head cocked on one side, listening for the sound of the water being poured into the basin. When he judged the right moment had come he would charge under the tent flap, invariably causing his victims to scream, while the more timid girls would bolt from the back of the tent, clutching bath towels round themselves.

The previous year Michael Tippet, my assistant, had also had a tame wildebeest calf that slept in a shed near his tent. But one night, when everyone was at dinner, a leopard broke into the shed and carried off the calf. In order to safeguard Oliver from such a horrible death I had an extension built on to the grass hut where I slept. It was made of stout poles, grass-thatched and completely enclosed with strong pig wire. The entrance was through my hut where the dogs slept, and I reckoned that they would give me warning if a leopard came during the night. As he grew older Oliver objected more and more strongly to being stabled at night and it became necessary to entice him inside by means of the bottle he had had as a baby, which he relished more than anything else.

When we left Olduvai at the end of the year it was a problem to know what to do with Oliver. Finally, Murray Watson, who had been studying wildebeest for his PhD thesis, offered to take him to the Serengeti Research Institute, which was then at Banagi in the Seronera Park. Murray hoped to set up a herd of tame wildebeest for observation and, in the next calving season, we caught two female calves as companions for Oliver. However, he resolutely refused to have anything to do with them. Like so many wild animals reared by hand, he saw no affinity between himself and his own kind.

As Oliver grew older his mischievousness did not decrease, but his size and weight increased at an alarming rate. After he had tossed a number of Africans by hooking his horns under the hems of their shorts, Murray thought of a preventive device. He fitted Oliver with half a bicycle tyre, attached at either end to the tips of his horns.

When he had been at Banagi for several months I went to visit him, and was greatly touched that he immediately recognized me. He nuzzled me and rubbed his forehead against me, inviting me to scratch him behind the ears. When I left, he tried very hard to squeeze himself into the Land-Rover beside me.

Latterly, at Olduvai, I have derived great pleasure from getting to know the wild birds and persuading them that my camp is a safe place. At present there is a red-backed scrub robin who regularly comes in for pieces of cheese. The habits of this species are described in the bird books as 'skulking in bush'. Probably for this reason, he hops across the floor of my living-room, over the dogs if they happen to be in the way, and perches on the rungs of chairs beneath the dining table. He has no fear whatsoever of the four Dalmatians, but became very angry when a brown mongrel dog, abandoned by the Masai, came to live in camp. He stood on the window sill chattering with rage and alarm, as he does when he sees a snake. He is aware that the supply of cheese is kept in the pantry, and if nobody is nearby he will fly to the laboratory and perch on the table, near to whoever is working there, to lead them back to the pantry and the cheese.

There is also a pair of white-naped ravens who have made my camp their headquarters for a number of years. They rear a family of three each year, in a nest perched in a vertical cliff, about three kilometres away. While the female is sitting, the male carries food and water to her from the camp – scraps of meat, broken dog biscuits or bits of cheese, which he dunks in the bird bath before carrying them away in order to supply her with liquid. As soon as the young birds hatch both parents work continuously, carrying food and water to the nest. In windy weather they are able to soar along the edge of the gorge nearly all the way to the nest and back again. The young ravens are brought into the camp as soon as they are capable of the three-kilometre flight. They are still gawky and not fully fledged when they first arrive. Their voices are particularly raucous and easily distinguished from their parents'. To begin with they are shy and unwilling to approach any of us closely, but they soon follow the parents' example and go anywhere in the camp. During the heat of the day the entire family usually rests and the birds groom themselves in the branches of the umbrella thorn in front of my living-room.

In 1978 an unusually interesting relationship sprang up between the three Dalmatian bitches and the young ravens. Dalmatian bitches habitually regurgitate food for puppies when they are being weaned. Not only the mother does this, but any other bitches living in the 'family'. It seems that our bitches consider the ravens as the young of our family who need to be fed, and all three have regurgitated small amounts of their food for them, which the young ravens have immediately flown down from the tree and eaten. So far as I have been able to observe, the Dalmatians' reaction to the ravens is triggered off by the young birds' raucous calls for food.

Each year, when the young birds are fully fledged and capable of feeding themselves, they are driven out of the area by the parents, who are relentless and never permit them to return to the territory they occupy themselves. I have not yet discovered the extent of an area occupied by a pair of ravens, but it seems to be of considerable size. Once a year the territorial rules are relaxed and the ravens from all around meet in a convocation. On three occasions this has occurred in April, during the rains. It seems that all the ravens, from far and near, young and old alike, gather together for the purpose of choosing mates. Ravens are monogamous and happily married pairs remain together although they join the convocation; but a bird who has lost his or her mate during the course of the year will acquire a new partner at this time. (This was demonstrated by the male of the Olduvai pair, whose first partner disappeared after becoming very lame. He reappeared with a younger raven after the annual convocation.) At the convocation, I have seen as many as sixty or seventy ravens flying together, soaring in the rising air along the edge of the gorge near camp. They perform aerobatics, play together in pairs by tossing objects to one another, and carry out most graceful and perfectly timed manoeuvres, rolling on their backs and doing half rolls, face to face, then extending their feet to touch one another before resuming normal flight.

Recently there was a near-tragedy in the raven family. One of the nestlings fell from the cliff-side nest and was incapable of flying up again, although he could flap his wings enough to flop along the ground. After much debating, because we were reluctant to interfere, my assistant, Peter Jones, decided to rescue the young bird and hand-rear it until it could fly. He climbed down into the ravine and brought it back to camp, where it was established in one of the guest rooms. The parents were infuriated when it was removed and dive-bombed Peter repeatedly. In order that they should not forget that the youngster was one of theirs we let it out of the guest house daily, when they were in camp. After a week Peter observed that the two young birds remaining in the nest had begun to fly, so he returned our visitor to the nest. He was immediately accepted and fed by the parents.

My present camp supports a number of wild creatures, many of whom visit us under cover of darkness, when we do not disturb them. There is a pair of genet cats who come for food each night. We leave milk, bananas and meat out for them. Their first choice is bananas, as long as they are fully ripe and sweet: they will not touch any that are slightly unripe. Food is also put out nightly for a family of black-tipped mongooses – small dark brown mongooses who mostly emerge at night. Recently a porcupine has also become a regular visitor, and the plate of broken dog biscuits, milk and bananas prepared for the mongooses is now topped with three raw potatoes, which seem to be the favourite food of the porcupine. However, he carefully pares off the skin, in thin slivers, before eating the potatoes.

There are also many birds that come to a bird bath made from an old lorry tyre cut in half. They come particularly during the dry season, when great flocks of canaries, sparrows, starlings and love birds fly in to drink and bathe. For a while a pair of pied wagtails were permanent camp residents and established their position of authority over the other birds by the strength of their personalities. They were very greedy for the grated cheese that was put down for them in the morning and at lunch time. Should we forget, or be unduly late, they would follow us about and sing their loudest to attract our attention. The female was so fearless that she also regularly came into my hut in the early morning and searched all over the floor for ticks that might have dropped off the dogs during the night.

A multitude of little field mice live in burrows round the camp and subsist largely on crumbs, left-over dog food and dog biscuits. They venture out from their burrows with much trepidation and finally seize dog biscuits only a little smaller than themselves, which they manage to carry away. This abundant rodent population has attracted a number of snakes from time to time, mostly spitting cobras. We are warned of their presence by the birds, who gather in flocks above the snakes, giving shrill alarm calls. Some of the staff have become adept at dispatching the cobras with catapults, and we have also been helped by the black-tipped mongooses.

The National Geographic Society of Washington DC has been almost entirely responsible for funding the work at Olduvai from 1960 onwards.

In March 1963 the first steps were taken to provide facilities for visitors to Olduvai. I wrote a small explanatory pamphlet which was printed locally. Thanks to the generosity of the National Geographic Society this was soon superseded by the illustrated pamphlet which is available today. Discussions were also held with Mr Hamo Sassoon, who was Conservator of Antiquities at the time, and it was decided to enrol three men to act as guides or guards, who would accompany visitors to the gorge, explain the various sites and prevent specimens being removed. During 1963 403 people visited the gorge, in 1972 the figure had risen to over 23,000 and in 1976 to 26,000.

As well as employing guides, it was decided to build

protective sheds over three sites so that visitors would be able to see the stone artefacts and fossil bones in their original positions, as they had been left by prehistoric man. This method of exhibiting sites had been used successfully in Kenya, particularly at Olorgesailie. It is clearly more interesting to see specimens in their original context than behind glass in a museum case. At the time there was very little money available for these buildings and they had to be constructed as cheaply as possible from corrugated iron, covered with a grass thatch. They were not particularly sightly, nor effective in keeping out the rain; but now, thanks to the generosity of Mr Gordon Hanes, it has been possible to replace them with permanent stone buildings.

As an archaeologist I am particularly appreciative of the Tanzania Government Antiquities Ordinance, which came into force in 1964. This forbids the removal of any stone tools or fossils from protected areas without the explicit permission of the Government. Formerly many important sites were despoiled by collectors before the fossils and tools could be studied in their original geological and stratigraphic context. In the past, too, no law prohibited the removal of specimens from their country of origin. As a result, institutions and museums that contributed funds towards field work expected a proportion of the finds in return. This meant that tools and fossils from a single site might be distributed in England, America, France or elsewhere. Subsequent study of this material thus became very difficult and very costly.

My licence to excavate at Olduvai is contingent on the fossils and tools remaining in Tanzania. Material may still be loaned overseas for study, provided it is returned within a reasonable period of time. This seems to me a wholly admirable arrangement.

We had planned for some time to set up a small museum at Olduvai, but it was not until 1970 that funds became available to install the exhibits. The building itself has been financed by the National Geographic Society on the under-standing that subsequent expenses would be met by the Tanzania Government. During 1970 Mr A. A. Mturi, Director of Antiquities, was able to divert part of his grant for furnishing the museum. A further grant was made from the Wallace Genetics Foundation through the kind offices of Mrs Leslie Douglas, of Washington, DC.

After I had drawn up the plans Mr Mturi arranged for technicians from the National Museum in Dar es Salaam to come to Olduvai and construct the cases and wall panels. Casts of the more important hominid fossils, stone tools and mammalian fossils were prepared by the staff at the Centre for Prehistory in Nairobi, who worked continuously on the project for several months. While I was mounting the exhibits I was most fortunate in having the assistance of Mrs Irene Brendeis and Mrs Judith Shackleton. Before her marriage Irene Brendeis stayed at Olduvai for some time, making a photographic study of the birds, insects and flowers found in the district. By remarkable good fortune Judith Shackleton was an artist by profession and her skill was invaluable in preparing some of the exhibits. Both these friends worked to the point of exhaustion in order to open the museum to the public by January 1971.

The Tanzanian Antiquities Department had meanwhile built a store to house the specimens excavated at Olduvai from 1969 to 1972. This also provides working space to study the material, so that I have been able to undertake analysis of the stone tools and fossils in camp instead of packing everything up for transport to Nairobi.

Until 1971 all visitors' fees were paid into the Research Fund, but these monies are now handled by the Ministry of

Culture and Youth on the understanding that all expenses incurred in providing facilities for visitors are paid by the Ministry, from the Olduvai revenue. Thus, the Research Fund no longer benefits from the entrance fees and, in order to supplement the research grant, books, postcards, slides etc., are sold to visitors at the entrance to the gorge.

CHAPTER THREE
Geology, Dating and Digging

THE LANDSCAPE seen by the visitor at Olduvai today is in many ways similar to that seen by early man, with the important exception that in early times a lake occupied what is now the central part of the gorge.

The present drainage into the gorge is from the west, but during prehistoric times it was from the volcanic highlands that lie to the south and east of Olduvai. This range of mountains consists of Lemagrut to the south and Olmoti to the east, with the immense caldera or subsidence crater of Ngorongoro between the two. We know that both Lemagrut and Ngorongoro had become extinct when Olduvai was occupied by early man, since their most recent lavas are older than the earliest Olduvai sediments; but Olmoti was still active, as was Kerimasi, another volcano to the north-east. These two volcanoes were responsible for erupting large masses of volcanic ash, which was deposited in the Olduvai area by the prevailing wind. More recently, the still-active volcano of Oldonyo Lengai – which lies to the north of Olmoti – has also been responsible for ash-falls in the area. The excellent state of preservation of many fossil bones at Olduvai is due in large part to rapid burial under falls of volcanic ash.

To the north-east of the gorge there is a range of Precambrian hills known as Oldonyo Ogol. These are part of the very old basement complex system of rocks which underlies the volcanic lavas and sediments, and they supplied early man with some of the raw materials from which he made his tools.

The discoveries relating to early man have all been made in the side gorge and in the eastern twenty kilometres of the gorge, where the deposits reach a thickness of seventy-five to ninety metres. At the base of the sequence is a rock known as a welded tuff. This is a volcanic ash which was erupted at such high temperature that it fused and became rock-hard when it came to rest on the ground. The welded tuff is widespread in the western part of the gorge and has been named the Naabi ignimbrite. It is visible in only one place in the eastern part of the gorge, where a fault running transversely across the gorge has cut through the lava that elsewhere overlies the welded tuff. Above the welded tuff is a series of lavas derived partly from Olmoti volcano and partly from an unknown source to the south of the gorge. They have been dated to 1.89 million years. Prehistoric man occupied the area soon after the lava flows, and the earliest fossil sites are just above it, or even resting on its surface.

Faults connected with the Great Rift Valley cut through the Olduvai beds in many places. The principal faults were originally numbered one to five by Professor Reck in 1913, but many additional faults have now been identified. Faulting began perhaps 1.7 million years ago, and continued intermittently until about 50,000 years ago. A severe phase of faulting took place 30,000 to 100,000 years ago, during which the north-west foothills of Ngorongoro subsided and formed the Olbalbal Depression.

The non-specialist may not realize how important a part geology plays in the work of archaeologists. Every archaeologist hopes to find a sequence of sites in a given locality that will reveal change and development through time. The geologist's first task is to place the sites in correct sequence. This is simple if the rock strata are clearly superimposed like the layers in a cake, with the oldest at the bottom. But the picture is usually more complicated on account of earth movements and erosion, so that great skill is needed to get the true picture.

The second task of geologists and geophysicists is to assign ages to the rocks in order to permit world-wide comparisons and possible correlation of evolutionary development. This is at once the most difficult and the most exciting part of research on early man. The two available approaches are palaeontology and geophysical methods. The latter are capable of assigning an age in years and are sometimes known as 'absolute dating'. They include radioactive dating by the potassium-argon method and geomagnetism, both of which are described later in this chapter.

Only a few rocks are suitable for dating by the potassium-argon process, but fortunately these occur at crucial points in the Olduvai sequence, near the beginning of the record. It is of historical interest to note that Olduvai is the first archaeological locality where potassium-argon dating was used. When Professor Garniss Curtis of the University of California at Berkeley presented his initial results, indicating that *Australopithecus boisei* (*Zinjanthropus*) and the earliest stone tools were more than 1.7 million years old, there was widespread disbelief and a general conviction that the date could not be right. But it is now generally accepted that this date is correct and that the first hominids and stone tools are earlier than anyone had guessed prior to the results from Olduvai. ('Hominid' means belonging to the family of man, the Hominidae.) Now still earlier hominid fossils are known from other sites in East Africa, and the date of the first tools probably goes back to just over two million years.

Another very important role for geology is to reconstruct the ancient environment in which the early hominids lived. Was it arid or tropical? Were there lakes and rivers nearby? What kind of plants and animals existed? The record at Olduvai is unusually complete and many aspects of the ancient environment are now known. Hominid fossils and stone tools occur almost continuously through the whole sequence of fossil-bearing rocks in the gorge. Olduvai, in fact, provides the longest record of early man that has yet been found; from nearly two million years ago until the present time.

Five different methods of dating have been used for Olduvai. These are potassium-argon or K/Ar, fission track, geomagnetism, racemization of amino acids and carbon 14. In the first three methods the deposits in which the specimens were found are dated, but in racemization and carbon 14 tests are carried out on the actual bones.

The potassium-argon method of dating consists of measuring the extent to which potassium 40 has been converted into calcium 40 and argon 40. Since the tests can be applied only to minerals that contain potassium, not to the actual fossil bones, it is of primary importance to obtain rock samples that have minerals contemporary with the time of deposition and that have not been incorporated from other sources. In the early days of dating the Olduvai sequence several erroneous dates were obtained as a result of testing rocks that contained minerals of different ages. Equally, since the tests are not made on the bones themselves, it is essential to date deposits that are as contemporary as possible with the fossils or artefacts that they contain.

The fission-track method, where it has been applied to samples from Olduvai, has fully corroborated the results obtained by potassium-argon. I am indebted to the late Dr W. W. Bishop for the following explanation of the process:

This method of dating is applied to natural glasses such as pumice or obsidian that are uranium-rich. The main isotope (U.238) decays by spontaneous fission at a rate of 10–16% per year, so that if the proportion of uranium atoms that have 'fissioned' in a sample are counted, it is possible to tell the age. The 'fissions' leave marks in the form of narrow tracks of intense damage. The damaged areas are then etched out so that the etch pits can be counted under a microscope. However, the rate at which the tracks accumulate in any mineral depends upon the uranium content, so that it is not sufficient just to count their abundance; the ratio of tracks to uranium content must also be established. This is done by exposing the sample to an artificial, measured dose of slow neutrons in a nuclear reactor, which causes fission of another isotope, U.235. Since the ratio of this isotope to U.238 is known, as well as the amount of artificial neutrons, if the artificial and natural tracks are counted a complicated formula will show the ratio of natural tracks to uranium content. Then, since the rate of uranium decay is known to be constant, the age of the sample can be determined.

Geomagnetic or palaeomagnetic dating is based on the fact that the earth's magnetic field changed positions from time to time in the past. These periods of reversed and normal polarity have been dated from geomagnetic studies of volcanic rocks with known potassium-argon ages. The earliest changes in polarity go back many millions of years and only the more recent concern the Olduvai story. The latest

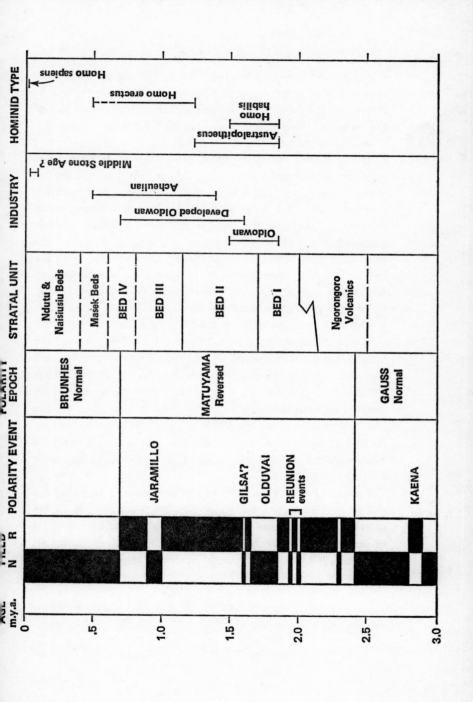

major period during which the north and south poles were reversed was from 2,430,000 to 700,000 years ago, and is known as the Matuyama Epoch. After this the positions of the poles are believed to have remained normal except for relatively short periods.

When a deposit is strongly magnetic it is sometimes possible to determine whether its polarity is normal or reversed by measuring it in the field by means of a portable magnetometer. For more accurate analysis it is necessary to remove a sample and measure it in the laboratory. The simplest method of obtaining a sample is to place a compass on part of the rock that can be detached easily and mark the existing north. The sample is then sent to the laboratory where it sometimes has to undergo complicated processing before the correct polarity can be determined.

Dating by racemization of amino acids is used in conjunction with radio-carbon dating. It is based on the rate at which various amino acids such as isoleucine aspartic acid have become racemized since a known date, obtained by carbon 14. Once this is established, it is possible to extend the dating backwards to specimens from the same locality that are too old for accurate radio-carbon dating. Since the rate of racemization is affected by temperature it is necessary to estimate past temperatures on the basis of present-day averages.

Carbon 14 dating can only be applied to specimens that are not more than 60,000 years old. Beyond that date it becomes unreliable. At Olduvai, therefore, where most of the material to be dated is between two million and seventeen thousand years old, it has a very limited use except where it is used as a basis for amino-acid dating.

* * *

46

One of the most common questions asked by visitors to Olduvai after they have seen the gorge is: 'How do you know where to dig?' Some people are under the impression that we sink large, deep holes down into the deposits on a hit-or-miss basis, hoping to strike an archaeological level by luck. This, of course, is not the case. By great good fortune the gorge has cut through an appreciable length of the old lake shore, where the hominid populations lived. In the areas to the north-west, where the gorge cuts through the central part of the old lake basin, the deposits contain neither artefacts nor fossils.

Sites are usually found by searching up and down the sides of the gorge and its subsidiary gullies, and noting areas where artefacts and fossil bones have eroded out on to the surface. It is generally possible to determine fairly accurately the level from which they have derived by marking the position of the pieces that are highest on the slope. If the artefacts or fossil bones appear to be of sufficient interest to merit an excavation, a trial trench about one and a half metres wide is cut into the slope. This is usually excavated in a series of steps. After the archaeological level has been identified and possibly other levels of interest, the trench is extended in whichever direction seems the most promising. This often entails the removal of some overburden. When this has been completed, the area is marked out by means of fifteen-centimetre nails into a grid of one-metre squares. Excavation within each square then proceeds in ten-centimetre spits, any change in the nature of the deposits being noted. As the finds are uncovered they are numbered while still in place, and their positions are plotted on graph paper. They are then lifted and taken back to camp, where they are entered in the site register after being cleaned and provisionally identified.

Picks and shovels are used for removing overburden, but digging of the archaeological levels is carried out by means of a special tool made in camp by the African workmen. This consists of a fifteen-centimetre nail beaten at the tip to a chisel point and hafted in a wooden handle with a right-angle bend that fits comfortably into the palm of the hand. The soil that has been excavated is swept up with brushes and hand shovels into shallow metal basins, known as *kerais*, for removal to the sieves. Any objects recovered in the sieves are labelled with the appropriate grid square and spit number unless they are of particular interest, in which case they are given individual numbers and entered in the register. When a site that has yielded hominid remains is being dug the deposit is generally washed after being dry-sieved. Small fragments of teeth or bone can easily escape detection if they are coated in clay.

Among the most useful adjuncts to excavation at Olduvai are cans of a standard size that have contained meat or other rations. Each digger keeps a can handy into which he puts objects that are too small to plot or that have been accidentally displaced. The sievers also place their finds in these cans, which fit neatly into trays for transport back to camp.

The different types of sites at Olduvai where archaeological and faunal material have been found can be subdivided as follows:

1 Living floors, in which occupational debris, including artefacts and food debris, is found on an old land surface or palaeosol throughout a depth of only a few centimetres.
2 Butchery or kill sites, where remains of a large animal such as an elephant or a herd of smaller animals are found in swamp deposits associated with artefacts.
3 River or stream channels, where occupational debris has become incorporated in the filling of an old water course.
4 Sites with diffused material where artefacts and faunal

remains are found throughout a considerable thickness of fine-grained sediments.

5 Localities with material sparsely scattered on an old land surface.

Excavations have been carried out at a number of sites that fall under the first three headings, i.e. living floors, butcheries and stream channels. In most cases the existence of a site was indicated by material washed out on to the surface of the slope below the *in situ* level. When undisturbed living floors on palaeosols have been uncovered, much information is usually gleaned. Butchery sites have also proved informative, but river channels, where the material is in a disturbed context, although often yielding an abundance of remains, have been unrewarding.

The gullies and other localities at Olduvai that have yielded fossils or artefacts are designated by the initials of the person who first recorded them, followed by the letter K for *korongo* – the Swahili word for gully – or the letter C for cliff.

CHAPTER FOUR
The Beds

PROFESSOR RECK, who was the first to study the geology of Olduvai on the German expedition of 1913, identified five main series of deposits, which he named Beds I to V. His system has continued to be used with certain modifications: Bed IV is now subdivided into two distinct units, known as Bed IV and the Masek Beds; Bed V has been subdivided and renamed the Ndutu and Naisiusiu Beds. The following outline of the geology is based on notes kindly supplied by Dr Richard L. Hay of the Department of Geology and Geophysics, Berkeley, California, who has made a detailed study of the geology.*

BED I

This is the lowest series of deposits in the sequence. It consists of layers of tuffs (volcanic ash) and claystones which in present-day geological parlance would be more correctly termed a formation. It was originally defined by Reck to include the sedimentary deposits above the lava (basalt), up to a marker bed that is known as Tuff IF. This tuff

---

* *Geology of the Olduvai Gorge* by Richard L. Hay, University of California Press, Berkeley, 1976.

has been retained as the upper limit of Bed I, but the lava has now been included, since this was the only practical method by which a lower series of deposits, which are below the basalt in the north-west part of the gorge, could reasonably be included in the sequence. As re-defined, therefore, Bed I consists of a lower sedimentary series (below the basalt), the basalt itself, and the sediment above it.

The lower sedimentary series, so far, has not yielded many fossils or much archaeological material. The sediments of Bed I above the basalt vary in thickness from twenty to forty-six metres and are made up of ash falls erupted from Olmoti, alternating with layers of clay. The deposits of volcanic ash are noticeably coarser and thicker at the eastern end of the gorge, towards their source. Bed I lasted for a relatively short time, in the geological sense, probably not more than 300,000 years, from about 2 to 1.7 million years ago. This date places it in the period known as Lower Pleistocene. The sediments of Bed I above the lava, which contain the fossil and archaeological remains, have been more extensively dated by potassium-argon than any other Lower Pleistocene stratigraphic unit. These tests, supplemented by the palaeomagnetic results, indicate that the fossil-bearing sediments probably span a period of no more than 150,000 years.

The living sites uncovered in Bed I during the 1960s were the oldest known at that time. Their chief importance lies in the fact that they demonstrate that nearly two million years ago man had already reached a stage of social structure which included communal centres where groups gathered together, built shelters and ate food. The living sites also provide the only evidence as to the diet and potential hunting ability of man at that time. Until recently it was not considered likely that the stage of owning a 'home' had been reached in the Lower Pleistocene: but the evidence from

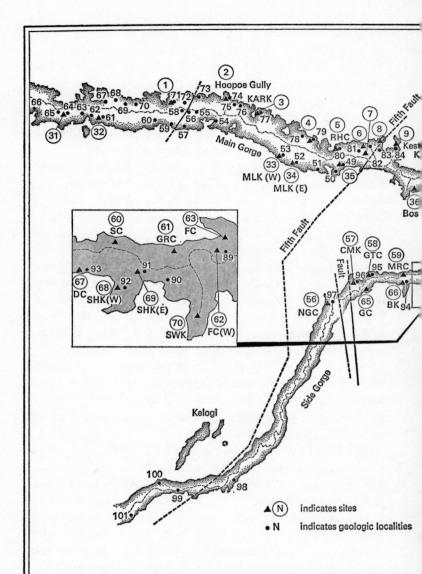

Sketch map of Olduvai Gorge to show the positions of the sites and geologic localities.

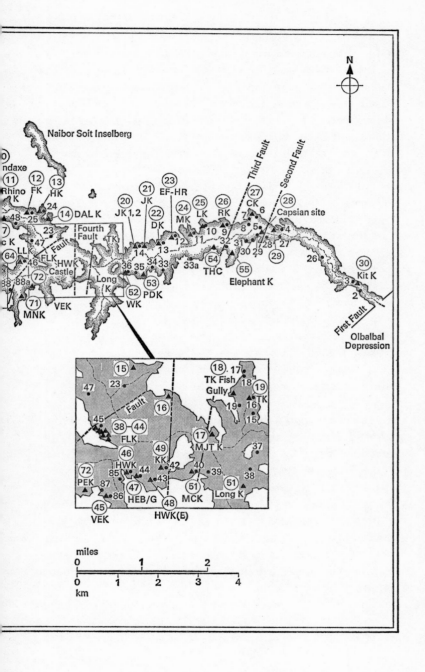

Olduvai has proved conclusively that this was so.

Living floors occur throughout the Olduvai deposits, but the best preserved are in Bed I, when man lived on the flats around the shore of the lake. When the lake rose the sites were often covered over quickly by lake sediments, before there had been time for the debris left behind to become weathered or disturbed. At this time, faulting had not yet begun to affect the area.

Four sites in Bed I have proved of particular interest. These are DK, which is between 1,900,000 and 1,750,000 years old; FLK NN, where the type specimen of *Homo habilis* was found in 1960; FLK, where the skull of *Australopithecus boisei* was found, and FLK North, where a series of occupation levels was found at the top of Bed I.

DK is the earliest of these sites, followed by FLK NN, FLK and FLK North. But since it is now known that Bed I was of relatively short duration, the time gaps between the sites were probably not very great. These sites are on old, buried land surfaces, or palaeosols, in which the top few centimetres of the deposit have been exposed to weathering and root action which have broken it down into a soil.

In 1961 we began a dig in lower Bed I at *DK* (named after Donald McInnes, a palaeontologist who worked with Louis at Olduvai during 1931–2). We had noted many tools and fossil bones at this site, eroding from a level just above the lava, at the base of the Bed I sediments and overlain by tuff that had been dated at 1.75 million years. In January, during the Christmas holidays, our son Philip, who was then twelve years old, dug a small trial trench at DK and discovered enough artefacts and fossils to justify a larger excavation. It revealed an extensive living floor as well as a circular stone structure.

The site was situated beside the edge of the old lake and

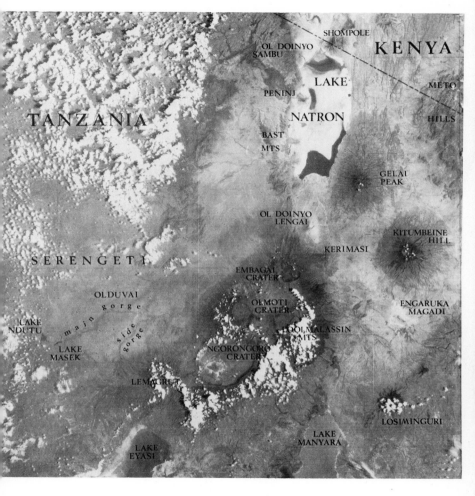

Satellite view of the eastern Serengeti and the volcanic highlands

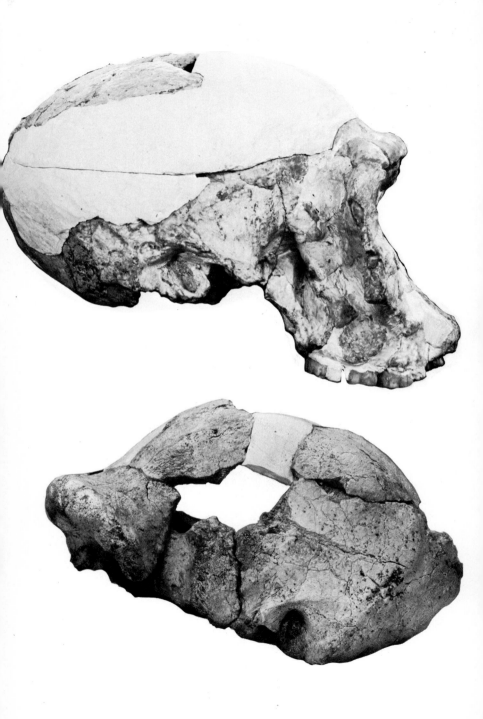

Above, left   Side view of the *Homo habilis* skull O.H.24 from Bed I

Below, left   The skull cap of *Homo erectus* from Bed II

Above   The skull of *Australopithecus boisei*, discovered by the author in July 1959

Excavations at the site where the skull of *Australopithecus boisei* was found

the occurrence of fossil rhizomes of reeds or papyrus in the deposits indicates that there was some vegetation along the shore in that area. The lake was certainly alkaline, in view of the presence of flamingoes. It can also be assumed that the shore sloped gently out to shallow water since flamingoes can only feed while wading through shallows in which there are rotifers and other micro-organisms on which they live. Part of the living floor was also on the surface of the basalt, where it rose into a hummock. It is possible that the spot was chosen by man as a conveniently dry area in the surrounding marshland.

At DK there is a stone circle which is the earliest man-made structure known. It is built of loosely piled blocks of lava and measures three and a half to four metres in diameter. It bears a striking similarity to crude stone circles constructed for temporary shelter by present-day nomadic peoples such as the Turkana in Kenya. These shelters are made by driving branches into the ground in a circle and placing stones round the bases to support them. The tops of the branches are bent inwards and interlaced, with grass sometimes placed on top. Both in present-day examples and at Olduvai more debris is found lying outside the huts than inside, since they are used mainly for sleeping, while cooking and eating and other activities take place in the open.

The Olduvai structure was a most surprising discovery in view of its age and for a while I was reluctant to believe that the blocks of lava had been artificially arranged into a circle. However, the geologists and prehistorians who have since seen the circle are almost unanimous in considering that it is likely to be the work of the early hominids and not a natural feature. To settle the question, we decided to uncover a much larger area of the DK living floor. In order to reach it we had first to remove about 1.5 metres of the overlying consolidated volcanic ash or tuff. It proved almost impossible to dig out by means of picks and shovels, since it had no natural cleavage planes. We therefore had to enlist the help of the Kenya Mines Department, who sent down one of their experts. He drilled holes in the tuff at intervals and then laid charges. All the while the stone circle alongside was unprotected, but the operation was so skilfully carried out that no damage was done. There was just enough force to crack through the tuff and break it into blocks which we were then able to remove by hand without further difficulty.

After the tuff had been removed we had to dig down through a further 1.5 metres of clay in order to reach the living surface. Only a few scattered fossils and artefacts were found in these levels, but when we came to the living floor we found many tools and fossil bones, although there was no trace of a second structure. By chance, the living floor in the area we cleared was on the surface of the lava, where it would have been impossible to erect a brushwood shelter, since there was no covering of soil into which the branches could be driven. Although we failed in our main objective of finding another hut circle, the tools and fossils that we found are the earliest known from Olduvai and are therefore of great importance.

At *FLK NN* (Frida Leakey Korongo, North-North, named after Louis's first wife, Frida) only part of the living floor was preserved. Former erosion, probably connected with the cutting of the gorge, had removed all the area to the east of the site, while the northern part was cut into by the present erosion slope. The first hominid tooth was found at this site at the end of May 1960 and we continued to find hominid remains at intervals until November, when Jonathan, my eldest son, discovered the mandible that became the type specimen for *Homo habilis*. All the remains were scattered over the surface of the living floor, where there were also large numbers of broken animal bones and a few stone artefacts. In all we found the remains of four hominid individuals at this site.

The remains uncovered on the living floor at *FLK*, where the skull of *Australopithecus boisei* (*Zinjanthropus*) was found in 1959, are very well preserved. None of the bones or artefacts shows any weathering or abrasion, and they were almost certainly buried rapidly by the lake silts. There appears to have been some orientation of oblong bone splinters such as might happen after a severe rain-storm, but the only serious disturbance of the remains likely to have taken place would have been that of scavenging animals, who may have gnawed the bones and moved them after the site was abandoned.

Although there was no structure preserved on this floor, a distinct pattern can be seen in the distribution of debris. Within an area of about 330 square metres that was excavated there was what appeared to be a central part, approximately six and a half by four and a half metres in diameter, where the bones had been smashed into very small fragments and where there were also innumerable small chips of quartz, many of which were too small to record on the plan. This part of the floor seems to represent the area where the maximum hominid activity took place, where stone tools were chipped and where bones were smashed open to obtain the marrow. Partially encircling this area on the windward side there was a zone about one metre wide where there were few bones or artefacts. Beyond this, in the marginal part of the floor, debris again became more plentiful, but contained very few small objects. It consisted mostly of natural cobbles, large artefacts and more complete bones. Such a distribution pattern might have resulted from a thorn fence or wind break being built round the windy side of the central area, over which the larger stones and more complete bones may have been thrown when they were discarded.

During August 1959, Dr R. Pickering, a geologist attached to the Tanzania Geological Survey who had been seconded to Olduvai for a few months, dug a test pit into the upper part of Bed I at a locality that came to be known as *FLK North*, between the main dig at FLK and Jonathan's site FLK NN. Large numbers of fossil bones and artefacts were found in this pit, and since they were from a level hitherto unexplored a trial trench was put in hand. The site proved extremely rich and much more extensive excavations were carried out during the following seasons. Five separate levels containing artefacts and fossil bones were uncovered just below the marker tuff at the top of Bed I. There was also a skeleton of an elephant embedded in clay, with a scatter of stone tools among the bones, probably representing a kill or butchery site. The only hominid bone found at this site was a terminal phalanx of the big toe, which almost certainly belongs to *Homo habilis*.

BED II

Unlike Bed I, Bed II spans a considerable period of time – probably 600,000 years. More changes took place in the stone industries, the hominid population and the fauna during Bed II than in any other period.

The deposits of Bed II extend vertically from the marker Tuff IF at the top of Bed I to the base of Bed III, the distinctive red bed, and are from twenty-one to thirty-five metres thick. They consist mostly of clays and sandstones

58

laid down either in the Olduvai lake or in streams that drained into the lake. The lower part of Bed II, below the Lemuta Member (a widespread marker bed, named after a locality near Olduvai, which consists of a windblown volcanic ash), compares closely with the upper part of Bed I and was clearly laid down under similar conditions, when both the fauna and the hominid population were still similar to those of Bed I. Just after the Lemuta Member a marked change took place in the fauna. The reason for the change is not fully understood, but the draining of the Bed I lake, brought about by the onset of faulting, may have been a contributory factor. Certain groups of animals that are common in Bed I and in the lower part of Bed II do not occur after the Lemuta Member. The majority of the swamp-loving species such as the *Deinotherium* disappeared and were replaced by those favouring both riverine and open savannah conditions, such as the equids (members of the horse family) and hippopotami. Equally, most of the Bovidae (antelopes) characteristic of Bed I no longer occur and other forms take their place.

There seems to have been a considerable hominid population in the Olduvai area during Bed II times. The sites are mostly in middle and upper Bed II above the Lemuta Member, although there are a few sites and scattered artefacts in the deposits below. However the Bed II sites are seldom in the undisturbed condition found in Bed I.

The principal sites excavated in Bed II, considered in ascending order, are as follows:

HWK (Henrietta Wilfrida Korongo) is situated near the junction of the main and side gorges. It has yielded tools and faunal remains at a number of different levels, the earliest at the very base of Bed II and the latest just above the Lemuta

Member. The lowest level consisted of an occupation floor on a clay palaeosol containing tools. Above this, in a deposit of clay, some of the tools were made from chert, a material with a conchoidal fracture that resembles flint.

MNK (Mary Nicol Korongo) is in middle Bed II. Conditions at this site are difficult to interpret. There were layers upon layers of occupational debris, amounting to a total thickness of 1.2 metres and extending over an area of eighty-four square metres. No particular pattern of distribution could be seen, but it was evident that the focus of maximum concentration varied from level to level. Natural cobbles brought to the site by man (known as 'manuports') were particularly abundant. The extent of abrasion on the artefacts does not suggest that they were carried by water for any distance and it seems that human agency is probably responsible for the great accumulation of material. A possible explanation may be that the site was a favourite camping place, re-occupied on repeated occasions, perhaps at sufficiently long intervals for vegetation to have grown over the objects left behind on previous visits. If the manuports, for example, had still been available, it is difficult to understand why more and more were brought in at each successive level.

Although the sources of all the principal types of rocks used for making stone tools have now been identified, the only actual quarry known is a site in the side gorge where the chert nodules were exploited by early man. The chert occurs in a horizontal band, in a small cliff at the mouth of MNK. It is in the lower part of Bed II, three to three and a half metres above the top of Bed I and at about the same stratigraphic level as chert artefacts at other sites. The nodules vary greatly in shape: some are thin and shelly, but the most sought-after by early man were substantial lumps from which good-sized flakes could be knocked off. The fact that man had worked the chert bed at this particular spot can be recognized by the number of broken nodules and flakes as well as anvils and hammerstones of gneiss and lava that were left behind. The area excavated at this site measured no more than eight by two metres, and the chert-bearing level was only about fifteen centimetres thick; but it yielded over 14,000 pieces that were numbered in place and entered on the plans, as well as an even larger number of very small fragments that were recovered by sieving.

The site known as *EF–HR* (Evelyn Fuchs – Hans Reck) is slightly later than MNK. It is on the north side of the gorge, above a limestone that overlies the Lemuta Member, and is not very extensive. An area of only fifty-four square metres was excavated. The artefacts consist mostly of handaxes, which were found lying on either side of a small, shallow stream channel. Faunal remains were unusually scarce and the only specimen of significance was the skull of an extinct giraffe, *Giraffa jumae*.

SHK (Sam Howard Korongo) is in the upper part of middle Bed II and is situated in the side gorge. It has yielded a great many artefacts and fossils as well as the shaft of a hominid femur, very severely weathered and pitted by corrosion (OH53).

TK (Thiongo Korongo) is in upper Bed II. Louis dug a small trench there in 1931 and found a series of handaxes made on slabs of white quartzite. When we made more extensive excavations there in 1963 we found that there were two distinct levels of human occupation, in which the tools were markedly different. Both levels contained handaxes, but while those in the lower level were similar to the large quartzite specimens that Louis had found, the upper contained small, poorly-made lava specimens, recalling those from the BK site, also in the upper Bed II.

The lower occupation surface at TK seems to have been situated alongside a small stream that was probably slow-moving and stagnant, judging by the nature of the sediments filling the channel. We found large numbers of waste flakes and broken bones lying in the bottom of the channel, but virtually no tools, suggesting that even in Bed II times man was in the habit of dumping waste into streams and that river pollution is no new phenomenon.

The most recent site in Bed II is *BK* (Bell's Korongo), consisting of a river channel 2.5 metres deep and relatively wide, although the exact width is not known. It is one of the richest sites in the gorge and has yielded many thousands of artefacts, as well as a deciduous molar and canine of *Australopithecus boisei* and an extensive collection of faunal remains. During the short-term excavations undertaken in the 1950s it had not been possible to interpret the stratigraphy with certainty. It was believed, however, and later fully confirmed by trenches dug during 1963, that the site represented an old river channel. It also became evident in 1963 that the channel filling could not be subdivided into any sequence, although it contained a vast number of fossil bones and artefacts throughout its depth.

Many of the tools and bone fragments are so fresh in appearance and their edges so sharp that they could not have been carried for any distance by the river. Man, therefore, must have lived close by, perhaps along the banks. Flash floods may have swept the debris from the living sites into the river bed, but the water probably subsided before the debris had been transported very far. Evidence for the occurrence of flash floods is confirmed by the resemblance of the sediments in the BK channel to those in the bed of the present Olduvai River, which is dry for most of the year but subject to sudden floods during the rains. When the foundations of the dam dug by Louis in 1965 exposed deposits in a section across the river bed, down to the underlying lava, they consisted of interbedded lenses of fine and coarse-grained sediments, similar both in consistency and in pattern of deposition to those in the BK channel.

Near the main river channel at BK there was a second, smaller channel that was probably a muddy, sluggish backwater. Remains of a number of large mammals were found in this channel. They were associated with stone tools, so the animals may well have been driven into the swamp by man. Horn cores and bones of the giant buffalo-like *Pelorovis oldowayensis* were the most numerous and included one almost complete skeleton found in an upright position, with stone tools scattered around it. Other remains included those of *Sivatherium, Elephas recki* and a number of the giant pigs that are characteristic of middle and upper Bed II.

BED III

This is a conspicuous red bed that can be seen in the eastern part of the main gorge and in the side gorge. It represents a period when the area was only sparsely populated by early man. The deposits consist of clays, sandstones and conglomerates (pebbles and cobbles cemented together) six to ten metres thick. They were laid down by streams draining into small, intermittently dry lakes, quite unlike the permanent lakes of Beds I and II. The red colour was caused by a chemical reaction produced by alternate wetting and drying of brown sediments on alluvial fans that were alkaline with soda. (Similar red beds can be seen today forming on the shore of Lake Natron, where the conditions are comparable.)

This bed has yielded few fossils and only two living sites are known. Most of the stone tools found in Bed III have been isolated finds, so that there is little information about the human or animal life of the time. It seems, however, that the same tool-making traditions and fauna that are found in the upper part of Bed II continued into Bed III.

The site *JK* (Juma's Korongo), in Bed III, has yielded assemblages of artefacts that may be homogeneous, although they occurred in a coarse, fluvial sand and it is probable that they are of mixed origin. This site was partly excavated by Dr Maxine Kleindienst in 1962 but the report on the archaeology is still unpublished. I undertook further excavations at JK in 1970 and uncovered a curious complex of pits and associated runnels cut into the surface of a pink siltstone. These were first exposed in three-metre-wide trenches and were damaged before their significance had been appreciated. However, a parallel trench was then dug down to the surface of the siltstone, and the pits it contained were charted with meticulous care. The pits vary in diameter from about one metre to fifteen centimetres and in depth from about sixty centimetres to ten centimetres. Some have overhanging rims and there are a number of instances in which a later pit has been dug into an earlier one that had become partly filled in. There are sometimes grooves round the walls, generally horizontal and in groups of four. In other pits there are jagged scrapes and small holes that could have been made by jabbing with a sharp point. Some of the small pits could have been made by animals such as hippos or antelopes walking over the surface when it was muddy and picking up clods of wet mud on their feet. I have observed similar holes around the shores of Lake

Masek made by animals walking over a muddy area covered by a thin crust of dried soil. None of the pits has smoothly rounded walls such as there would be if they had been formed by water action.

A number of runnels, eight to fifteen centimetres deep and five to ten centimetres wide, with straight, vertical sides, connect some of the pits. Occasionally, the siltstone has been pushed upwards along the edges of the runnels, indicating that the deposit was soft at the time they were made. When exposed in cross section the bases of the runnels are seen to be flat and devoid of vertical cracks, showing that they are not natural fissures. A pair of runnels sometimes converge and lead into a pit, so that, if they are artificial, it seems likely that their purpose was to channel water into the pits. Like some of the pits, runnels have also been made at different times, with later ones cutting across earlier. In one area, two long convergent runnels are transected by two shorter ones that also converge and lead into a pit. It is evident that the two long runnels would have become useless for conveying water once they had been cut through by the second pair.

A considerable volume of siltstone has been dug out from the pits and removed from the site. The question thus arises as to whether the main objective was obtaining quantities of the deposit or the digging of the pits themselves.

This is clearly not a living site; but there is evidence that man was present, since flakes and bone chips were found in some of the pits. It may represent some domestic or cultural activity hitherto unrecorded in the early Stone Age. Extraction of salt immediately comes to mind as a possible interpretation. The siltstone is highly saline at present, but may not have been at the time that the pits were dug. However, assuming that it was, the salt could have been extracted by either of two methods, both of which

65

are practised in Africa today: by filling the pits with water to leech the salt out of the deposit, which could be collected later, when the water had evaporated and left it as residue; or else by removing the siltstone for extraction of the salt elsewhere, presumably at the living site. The first alternative would account satisfactorily for the runnels leading into the pits, but not for what appear to be marks of digging, still plainly visible on the pit walls. Had the pits been flooded, these marks must surely have become obliterated, unless they were made when the salt crust was removed.

Analysis of various samples from this site, kindly undertaken by Professor Peter Robins of the Department of Chemistry, Nairobi University, shows a much higher concentration of sodium chloride in the filling of a pit than in either the siltstone or the deposits above and below it. This is suggestive, and further sampling is required; but it is by no means conclusive, since the salt may have accumulated subsequently by ground water action or seepage after the site was used by man.

The purpose of these pits and runnels remains obscure, neither is it possible to determine what agency was responsible. In fact it is probable that more than one was involved if the purpose was to obtain salt or saline earth, a substance required by men and animals alike.

Absolute dating of the pits complex has not been possible, but on the geomagnetic evidence they appear to be well within the Matuyama Reversed Epoch, which came to a close about 700,000 years ago. Therefore, they are probably in the region of 900,000 years.

BED IV

This can only be distinguished as a separate bed in the eastern part of the gorge and in the side gorge, where Bed III is distinctive. Further west the division between the two beds is obscure and cannot be determined with certainty. In the eastern part of the gorge Bed IV is five to eight metres thick, but it becomes thicker to the west, particularly where it fills fault troughs. It is chiefly composed of clays, but also contains sandstones and conglomerates which were deposited by streams flowing through grassy plains into small intermittent lakes.

There are two tuffs (Tuff IVA and IVB) and one or more widespread siltstones that can be used for correlation in Bed IV. Four tool-bearing levels are known between Tuff IVA and the grey siltstones, all of which are earlier than Tuff IVB. There is also a series of sites in upper Bed IV above Tuff IVB, particularly on the south side of the gorge.

The faunal remains of Bed IV are usually fragmentary, but hippopotami, equids and crocodiles are common at nearly all sites. Catfish bones are also plentiful. In many respects the fauna stands close to that of upper Bed II, with the exception of the Suidae (pigs) and Bovidae, both of which are poorly represented and do not include the variety of species found in Bed II. It is not clear, at present, whether this is due to different ecological conditions or to other causes.

Sites in Bed IV are generally in river or stream channels, like some of those in Bed II. No site with artefacts is known where some degree of water action can be ruled out positively, although the fresh condition of many specimens suggests that the artefacts and bones could not have been transported for any great distances.

When work on Bed IV began, one of the first sites to be explored was *HK* (Hopwood's Korongo, named after the palaeontologist from the British Museum who accompanied the 1931 expedition), where nearly 500 handaxes and cleavers had been excavated in 1931. The small trench dug in 1969 was mainly intended to check the stratigraphic position of the site, since ample material had already been collected. It soon became apparent from their association with blocks of tuff from the Ndutu Beds, as well as pieces of calcrete (limestone), that the artefacts were not in their original context but had been deposited in a concentrated mass by more recent stream action.

Later in the year, similar conditions were revealed at another site supposedly in Bed IV, *TK Fish Gully* (Thiongo Korongo), where the late Dr John Waechter of the London Institute of Archaeology had first excavated in 1962. Here, too, the artefacts had been incorporated in a very recent deposit, also containing blocks of the Ndutu Beds. Thus, two of the sites that had yielded large collections of tools, believed to be from Bed IV, proved valueless for interpreting the cultural sequence.

HEB (Heberer's Gully, named after a German anthropologist) is in lower Bed IV and contains five distinct levels altogether. The lowest consists of a shallow stream channel about two metres wide which runs almost parallel with the present edge of the gorge. It contained a number of tools, some of which are in sharp condition, while others are much abraded. There is also considerable difference in size and form among the handaxes and it is probable that this level represents a mixed assemblage of artefacts, perhaps derived from different sites.

About thirty centimetres above the channel, at the eastern end of the site, there was an old land surface with a concentration of artefacts and fossil bones. Nearly all the handaxes are made from a fine-grained green phonolite, a high-quality rock for tool-making; they are among the most elaborately finished of any in Bed IV. Bone was also quite extensively used for tools at this level and there is a well-made handaxe of elephant bone, as well as one side of an elephant pelvis in which the acetabulum (the hollow into which the head of the femur fits) has been pounded, and evidently used as a mortar. At a slightly higher level, at the western end of the site, there is a third level consisting of a river sand that contained many boldly-flaked handaxes and some cleavers. They are almost entirely made of basalt and trachyandesite derived from Lemagrut, with a few specimens of white quartzite; the green phonolite so common at the underlying level is barely represented. These tools are all in an exceedingly sharp condition, in spite of the fact that they were in a river sand. The tools from the fourth level, also at the western end of the site and only at a slightly higher level, are very similar to the series from the third level. The fifth and uppermost level above the grey siltstone contained few tools.

In upper Bed IV above Tuff IVB, an area of seventy square metres was excavated at site *WK* (Wayland's Korongo, named after a former Director of the Geological Survey of Uganda). A hip bone and femur of *Homo erectus* were found here. When we excavated this site conditions seemed more favourable for preservation of evidence of structures than at any other in Bed IV, but in spite of a meticulous search no post holes or any other evidence of buildings could be discerned.

A little further to the east of WK, along the southern rim of the gorge, a hippopotamus skeleton was found in another channel that had cut down through Bed IV as far as the top of Bed III. Tools surrounded the skeleton, which belonged to an unusually massive specimen of *Hippopotamus gorgops*; this probably represents yet another butchery site, although there was no suggestion that the animal had died in a swamp.

Still further east, at *WK East* and *PDK* (Peter Davies Korongo) three trenches were dug into what is probably one fairly wide but relatively shallow river channel in upper Bed IV that appears to have been oriented in a south-east to north-west direction. In one trench, Tuff IVB had been completely cut out, but in the remaining two it had been only partially removed and was present at the base of the channel, although much reduced in thickness.

THE MASEK BEDS

These beds are named after Lake Masek, at the head of the gorge. Until the geology of the gorge was studied in detail they were considered to be part of Bed IV and for a time were known as Bed IVB. They consist mainly of two deposits of windblown (aeolian) ashes from the now extinct volcano Kerimasi. They are quite distinct from the underlying clays, sandstones and conglomerates of Bed IV and represent a drier climate. At the time when these beds were being deposited the Olduvai area was probably a dry grassy plain with some stream channels running through it. A proportion of these streams cut down through Bed IV into Bed III and the largest represents the earliest phase of the present gorge.

Only one living site of this period is known, at *FLK*, in the cliff overlooking the '*Zinjanthropus*' site. Part of a human mandible was found there by one of my African staff during 1969. This discovery led to 'follow-up' excavation that disclosed an extensive living site, although very few artefacts had been visible beforehand, either *in situ,* or on the slope below the cliff. The tools were in a shallow river channel, no more than forty centimetres deep and four metres wide. Numbers of elaborately trimmed quartzite handaxes, flakes and bone fragments lay within the channel and on the higher ground on either side of it. All the artefacts are in mint condition, and there appears to have been virtually no displacement of the material.

This site is stratigraphically between the two aeolian tuffs that make up the Masek Beds; it postdates the lower tuff, since blocks of this tuff are incorporated in the channel filling, but antedates the upper tuff, which overlies the northern part of the channel.

THE NDUTU BEDS

These deposits are named after the second lake at the head of the gorge. They were originally considered part of Bed V. An upper and a lower unit can be recognized within the Ndutu Beds. The latter is seldom preserved, although it has yielded a few important fossils. Richard Hay considers that the lower unit may extend back as far as the Middle Pleistocene, which began about 700,000 years ago; although the upper unit is certainly no older than the Upper Pleistocene and is probably 50,000 to 75,000 years old.

The fawn-coloured tuffs of the upper part of the Ndutu Beds were deposited after the gorge had been cut and remnants of these deposits can be seen adhering to the sides of the gorge in certain areas. Oldonyo Lengai, the still-active volcano to the north of the gorge, was responsible for erupting these ashes which formed into dunes after they were deposited on the plains. They eventually dispersed into a horizontal bed that can be seen beneath the uppermost deposits of limestone, where it has been cut through by erosion. A large proportion of the ash also drifted over the edge of the gorge and partially filled it. Subsidence of the first fault at the mouth of the gorge, which took place between 100,000 and 30,000 years ago, was responsible for a deeper excavation of the gorge and the removal of most of the Ndutu Beds.

THE NAISIUSIU BEDS

Another series of tuffs, superficially similar to the Ndutu Beds, and originally included in Bed V, is now known to be much more recent. It has been given separate status and termed Naisiusiu (a Masai word for the sound of wind rustling through dry grass, pronounced Nai-soo-soo). These beds generally consist of yellowish-fawn aeolian tuffs, also erupted from Oldonyo Lengai. They occur on the surface of the plains and in places within the gorge itself. Unlike the Ndutu Beds they are not affected by faulting, which must have ceased before they were laid down. Carbon 14 dates have been obtained on samples of ostrich eggshell and bone collagen from a late Stone Age living site in the Naisiusiu Beds near the Second Fault. The ostrich eggshell gave a figure of 17,000 BP and the bone collagen 17,500 ± 1000 BP. A calcrete that underlies the Naisiusiu Beds has given dates of 19–24,000 years.

CHAPTER FIVE
Finding the Hominids

THE HOMINID FOSSILS discovered at Olduvai, in other parts of East Africa, in South Africa and in Asia have greatly expanded our concept of man's evolution. Gradually palaeo-anthropologists are beginning to identify the various species of early hominids and to place them chronologically in relation to one another.

Since I first began to live most of the year at Olduvai a systematic search of the exposures for hominid and other fossils has been made at the end of each rainy season. At this time the fossils have been washed clean and can be seen much more clearly than when they are covered in dust during the dry season. Some important discovery has been made almost every year in the course of the annual search.

One of the most significant aspects of the work at Olduvai during the 1960s was the discovery that *Australopithecus boisei* lived side by side with an early species of *Homo*. This was later borne out by discoveries at East Turkana in Kenya.

The name *Australopithecus*, meaning 'southern ape', was given by Professor Raymond Dart to the first specimen ever found, a juvenile skull discovered in South Africa in 1924. Two distinct forms of *Australopithecus*, have since been identified in Africa: a gracile, lightly-built type known as

73

Australopithecus africanus (to which Dart's original specimen belongs); and a stocky, robust form – *Australopithecus robustus*. The gracile form does not seem to be represented at Olduvai; *Australopithecus boisei** resembles the robust form.

In all, three types of early hominids have been found at Olduvai: *Australopithecus boisei* (first called '*Zinjanthropus*'); *Homo habilis*, a small, lightly-built creature; and *Homo erectus*, a hominid whose brain capacity was considerably larger than the other two.

The remains of *Australopithecus boisei* are relatively scarce and consist only of the original skull, a fragment of thigh bone and several teeth; but they were found distributed over a wide range of deposits from Bed I to the top of Bed II, and therefore range between 2 and 1.1 million years old. Remains of *Homo habilis*, are far more common, although they have been found only in Bed I and lower Bed II – demonstrating that at this time *Homo habilis* and *Australopithecus boisei* were contemporaries. In upper Bed II times *Australopithecus boisei* lived side by side with *Homo erectus*, whose remains have not been found any lower than at this level.

It seems clear from the evidence at Olduvai that *Homo habilis* and *Homo erectus* did not overlap chronologically, and it is possible that they represent two stages in human evolution.

The discovery of the skull of *Australopithecus boisei* (*Zinjanthropus*) was one of the occasions when both perseverance and luck played a part. Despite the fact that we had found very few hominid remains on our early visits to Olduvai, Louis and I had remained firmly convinced that they would one day come to light, and we kept on looking.

---

* *Australopithecus boisei* was named after Mr Charles Boise, who for many years aided our work financially and also set up the Boise Fund in Oxford to assist in the study of early man.

On 17 July 1959 I was out hunting for fossils by myself, with my two Dalmatian dogs for company, while Louis rested in camp after a slight attack of flu. As I was working over the slopes of Bed I I suddenly saw the skull. I was doubtful, at first, whether it was hominid, since the mastoid region that was exposed was quite different from any I had seen in human skulls. Instead of being solid bone it was permeated with air cells, such as are found in skulls of particularly heavy animals, to compensate for excessive weight. However, after brushing away a little of the covering soil I saw two teeth that were unquestionably hominid. They were so large that I mistook them for molars, although they were, in fact, premolars (molar-shaped premolars are one of the characteristics of the robust *Australopithecus*). I was tremendously excited by my discovery and quickly went back to camp to fetch Louis. When he saw the teeth he was disappointed, since he had hoped the skull would be *Homo* and not *Australopithecus*.

When the skull had been partially exposed we found that it had been broken into a great many fragments, although all the pieces lay close together within an area approximately forty-five centimetres in diameter.

By good fortune a professional photographer, Des Bartlett, who was then working with the late Armand Denis, was due at Olduvai to take pictures of our work. We piled a cairn of stones over the skull to protect it from animals and waited impatiently for Des to arrive, so that he could make a complete photographic record as we uncovered and removed the skull. We began by carefully collecting all the pieces that were visible and then removed the surrounding soil to be sieved and later washed through finer sieves. The task of reassembling the fragments took many months, and it was not until three years after the discovery that the final reconstruction was carried out by Professor Phillip Tobias of the University of Witwatersrand, South Africa.

The Fourth Pan African Congress on Prehistory was to be held in Kinshasa, in what was then the Belgian Congo, during September of that year. We were due to attend, and our excitement over the discovery of the skull was so great that we had a special travelling box made and took it with us, holding it on our laps. Looked at afterwards, one can only regard this as quite irresponsible behaviour: we had no right to subject an irreplaceable fossil to the hazards of air travel. On our way to Kinshasa we stopped overnight at Johannesburg to show the skull to Phillip Tobias, to whom we had cabled cryptic messages in advance and who had then only recently taken over the Chair of Anatomy from Professor Dart. Phillip Tobias met us at the airport and we drove into the town in a state of mounting excitement, arriving at our hotel after midnight. We unpacked the skull on our dressing-table and Phillip's enthusiastic delight matched our own.

The Congress was held in the Jesuit University of Louvanium and we were billeted in the staff quarters, since it was then the long vacation. Louis and I were allocated a small sitting-room as well as our bedroom and we held a series of evening receptions for the skull, inviting only a few people at a time so that everybody had the opportunity to make a personal examination. Most appropriately, Professor Dart was with us and it was a great pleasure to show him our find. It was while we were still at the Congress that Louis and I decided to invite Phillip Tobias to undertake the study of the skull. The result has been his magnificent monograph, published in the second of the Olduvai volumes, which will stand for all time as a model of palaeo-anatomical studies.

We resumed work at Olduvai in February the following year, 1960, by putting in hand a major excavation at the site where the skull of *Australopithecus boisei* had been found. With a crew of about sixteen Wakamba workmen from Kenya we quarried out many tons of overburden in order to expose the deposits that had contained the skull. We had hoped to find the mandible; but, although an area of about 925 square metres was eventually uncovered, no further parts of *Australopithecus boisei* were found. A tibia and fibula (leg bones), some teeth and fragments of another skull from the same level came to light, but subsequently proved to belong to the lightly-built *Homo habilis*.

The discovery of *Homo habilis* was made by my eldest son, Jonathan, who was working with me at Olduvai after leaving school. While excavations were in progress at FLK, the *'Zinjanthropus'* site, Jonathan often wandered off to search for fossils elsewhere. One day he returned with a very strange mandible which he had found near FLK, on the slopes of Bed I. The mandible was later identified in the Nairobi Museum as the lower jaw of a sabre-toothed feline or machairodont, which is one of the rarest animals in the fauna of Olduvai. We immediately began a search for other parts. None came to light, but a single well-preserved hominid molar turned up most unexpectedly in the sieves. The discovery of the tooth led to extensive excavations, which proved to be among the most rewarding and exciting ever carried out at Olduvai. Jonathan directed the excavations and himself found the mandible and parietals which became the type of *Homo habilis* (OH7). (The hominids found at Olduvai are designated by the letters OH for Olduvai Hominid, followed by their number as far as possible in order of discovery.)

The name *Homo habilis* (handy man) was given by Professor Dart to the small hominid in view of his ability to make tools to a set and regular pattern. He must be considered as the tool-maker of Bed I, in preference to *Australopithecus boisei*, who seems unlikely to have progressed beyond a tool-using stage of development. The application of the word *Homo* to this group of hominids has been questioned. Some people would prefer the name *Australopithecus habilis*, conceding the ability to make tools, but for reasons of zoological nomenclature substituting *Australopithecus* for *Homo*. The original definition of *Homo habilis*, published in 1962, was based on incomplete material and is not entirely satisfactory. However, discoveries made since 1962 have confirmed that *Homo habilis* differs from *Australopithecus*, including the gracile type, in a number of significant respects and the name has come to be more and more widely accepted.

The building of a 'museum-on-the-spot' at site MNK led indirectly to the discovery of one of the most important hominid skulls, OH13. It proved to be the latest known example of *Homo habilis*. A workman named Ndibo Mbuika was collecting small stones to mix into concrete for the building, when he uncovered a human tooth, lying not more than a yard from the footpath we had used daily, going to and from the excavations. He did not report his discovery immediately, but covered the tooth with a little pile of stones and waited until next morning when he led Louis to the spot and showed him the tooth in place. It was a beautifully preserved hominid premolar. A clump of bushes and some grass were growing just above where the tooth lay; and when these were cleared away several fragments of skull were found on the surface, where they had lain hidden under the vegetation. Men with sieves were then brought to the site, the area marked out and the surface soil scraped up and sieved. Almost the whole of the lower jaw, part of the upper jaw and many fragments of skull were recovered within a short while.

When the staff returned from work that evening the news

The author supervises the sieving of soil from an excavation

The author cleaning the surface of the pink siltston in Bed III, in which pits and runnels were found

Louis Leakey shows Dr Melville Grosvenor, then President of the National Geographic Society, the skull of *Australopithecus boisei* and other hominid fossils from Olduvai

about the skull was quickly circulated. We were amazed when four men who had been working two kilometres or so further up the side gorge expressed no surprise at the news and told us that one of them, Musao Musombe, had 'seen' the discovery taking place and had described it to them in detail. This man had the appearance of being stolid and wholly unimaginative and it was surprising to find that he seemed to have this extra sensory gift. None of our workmen was impressed by the incident. They took it as a matter of course and were most astonished at our reaction. We knew that there had been no communication between the men at the two sites, and, moreover, the detailed descriptions that Musombe gave of the colour of the skull parts, how they had lain and how we had set about collecting them, were far too precise to have been transmitted by a verbal message.

A discovery that I made myself of part of a hominid mandible goes to show once again what an important part luck plays in the search for relics of early man. On this occasion I was transporting a large tin of paint from the camp to the museum, where we were preparing the exhibits. As usual, the four dogs were in the back of the car. When we came to the steep hill where the road descends into the gorge, the tin of paint began to slide on to the dogs. I stopped the car to secure the tin and, as it was on a steep slope and the brakes were not very reliable, I decided to place a stone under the wheel. When I bent down to pick up a suitable stone, I was amazed to see a hominid mandible with three teeth lying in the road next to the stone. Innumerable cars had travelled over the road since the present camp was opened in 1967 and it is most surprising that the mandible had suffered no damage. It was, of course, no longer in its original deposit, but the adhering matrix indicates that it was probably derived from a sandy conglomerate at a low level in Bed II.

During the 1968-9 season one of the African staff, Peter Nzube, found an almost complete cranium of *Homo habilis* at site DK in lower Bed I (OH24). The skull was fragmented and the pieces compressed and crushed flat, the whole being cemented together by a hard lime matrix that also covered the surface of all the pieces except for two small areas where the bone was exposed. The skull lay in an area that had been repeatedly searched for fossils, but nobody except Nzube had realized what the lump of limestone contained. Although this specimen had been found on the surface, it was possible to establish its stratigraphic position, since it lay on a deposit of clay just above the basalt and was overlain by a tuff dated at 1.75 million years. About thirty centimetres below the tuff there is a horizon of limestone concretions that are indistinguishable from those adhering to the skull, so that this can be assumed to be the original level from which it eroded. 'Follow-up' operations at this site consisted of removing the surface soil from the entire slope in the area where the skull had lain and washing it through fine sieves. A number of additional pieces were found, as well as parts of several teeth. Eventually, an area of approximately 100 square metres was cleared. There was evidence to show that the skull had eroded from the deposit many years ago; some pieces were near the parent block, on the present sloping surface, but others that had become detached much earlier had rolled downhill and were found buried beneath up to one metre of hillwash.

Five months were spent in the field searching for parts of this skull. When it reached the laboratory in Nairobi Dr R. J. Clarke spent another six months detaching the various fragments from one another and removing the extremely hard matrix, so that they could be reassembled. This was finally achieved in 1970, when Ron Clarke spent his summer vacation from London University working on the skull. Although the reconstruction is not entirely symmetrical and the vault is still slightly crushed downwards, the morphology can be seen quite clearly and indicates that the skull is probably of *Homo habilis*, with a strong possibility that it is a female.

Louis discovered a skull of *Homo erectus* (OH9) on 2 December 1960. He had been visiting various sites with a geologist, and while they were walking through the side gorge Louis noticed a small, insignificant gully that he believed had not been examined previously. He walked across to it the following morning and immediately noticed a little rounded mass of bones lying in the bottom of the gully, where Bed II was exposed. At first glance these seemed very similar to the bony carapace of a fossil tortoise. Since this resemblance had deceived us both on many occasions, Louis was wholly astonished to discover that on this occasion what appeared to be a tortoise was in fact a human skull. He rushed over to Jonathan's site, where I was working, and excitedly told me the news. We both then returned to the small gully and set about looking for additional pieces of the skull. Several fragments were lying near the original pile, including one of the brow ridges, which was unbelievably massive. We did not succeed in retrieving all the missing pieces, so that part of the vault has had to be reconstructed, but a sufficient amount is preserved for its shape to be deduced with reasonable accuracy.

Although the skull was found on the surface, the adhering matrix was sufficiently distinctive to determine from which level it had come. When this was excavated only a few quartzite flakes, some fish and mammalian bones were found, but no finished tools.

The cranial capacity of this skull has proved to be in the region of 1000 cubic centimetres. This is in marked contrast to the cubic capacity of a second skull (OH12) also attributed to *Homo erectus*, and found by my former daughter-in-law Margaret Avery in upper Bed IV. Although the skull is incomplete, enough is preserved to indicate that the cranial capacity was approximately 700 cubic centimetres. Both OH9 and OH12 were fully adult at the time of death. It is possible that they represent a male and a female. If so, very marked sexual dimorphism must have existed in *Homo erectus*.

An ulna (OH36), probably of *Homo erectus*, was found in January 1971, by Muia Mutala, then foreman of the excavations. It appeared to have eroded from a marker tuff near the top of Bed II, known as Tuff IID. Since the type of deposits suggested that other parts of the skeleton had probably not been dispersed by water action and might be found nearby, extensive excavations were made following this discovery. No further remains of *Homo erectus* came to light, however, although two incisors and a molar of *Australopithecus boisei* (OH38) were found at the same level. They were lying close together but without any accompanying bone. By present day analogy it seems possible that they may have been part of material regurgitated by a large carnivore such as a hyaena.

The first known pelvis of *Homo erectus* was found during the excavation of the site at WK in upper Bed IV, associated with an abundant Acheulean stone industry. Since then, a better preserved and more complete pelvis has been found at East Turkana; it bears a close resemblance to the specimen from Olduvai.

Altogether the few remains of *Homo erectus* so far found at Olduvai have revealed very little about his physical characteristics, his way of life, or, most important of all, his relationship to *Homo habilis*. In order to solve this latter problem, more work needs to be done in middle Bed II, where neither species has yet been found.

CHAPTER SIX
The Stone Tools

OLDUVAI IS UNIQUE among Lower and Middle Pleistocene sites in that the sources of nearly all the principal rocks used for making stone tools are known. A striking fact, which had not been appreciated until recently, is that some materials were transported considerable distances from their sources. Many of the 'heavy duty' tools were almost certainly manufactured, or at least blocked out, wherever the raw material occurred and then carried back to the living sites for final trimming. The rocks selected were generally fine-grained and homogeneous, since these are essential criteria for obtaining sharp-edged cutting or chopping tools; really sharp edges cannot be obtained with coarse-grained material and flaws make accurate flaking impossible.

The most common material found at the sites now exposed in the gorge is a white tabular quartzite from the Naibor Soit inselberg, just north of the junction of the main and side gorges. The source of this quartzite is closer to most of the sites than any of the other rocks used, and this probably explains its abundance at nearly all sites throughout the Olduvai beds.

The lavas used in Bed I for making choppers and other heavy duty tools were available to early man in the form of rounded water-worn cobbles, obtained from streams draining into the lake from the volcanic highlands to the south-east. A favourite lava was a green nephelinite. Cobbles and pebbles of this rock can now be found in streams draining down from Sadiman, a volcano immediately east of Lemagrut. The lavas from Lemagrut were also widely used.

Chert, a form of silica that is as sharp and as easily flaked as flint and of similar composition, became available for a while at about the time of the Lemuta Member in the lower part of Bed II. It was principally used for making small tools. Its superiority over all the materials available until then seems to have stimulated the manufacture of small tools and given rise to a wider range of tool types and a proportionate increase in the total tool-kit. Deposits of chert occur naturally in Beds I and II at Olduvai. At the quarry site in Bed II, where early man dug out the nodules and left behind some flakes and hammerstones, the chert nodules have a wide variety of forms; but the solid, substantial pieces were the most sought-after by early man, since it was possible to detach serviceable flakes from them. Some of the smaller nodules were also used for making miniature chopping tools in which the projecting parts of the nodules were trimmed, so that there were a number of short, sharp edges.

The formation of chert in alkaline lake deposits at Olduvai and elsewhere has been the subject of a prolonged study by Richard Hay. He has kindly supplied the following note:

The origin of the chert was only recently discovered. It forms only in soda or alkaline lakes with high concentrations of sodium carbonate, such as Lake Magadi in Kenya and Lakes Natron and Manyara in Tanzania. In these lakes sodium combines with silica which is brought into the lakes by rivers, to form rare sodium-silicate minerals such as magadiite. These are deposited as extensive layers over the bottom of the lakes. By processes not yet fully understood these layers lose their sodium and water and are transformed into nodules of chert whose chemical composition is SiO_2.

Chert can form by this process in only ten thousand years, unlike the cherts of Europe which require millions of years to form. The chert at MNK, in the side gorge, formed in mud along the southern margin of a large lake. When the water level dropped the chert was exposed and used by early man.

Above the Lemuta Member, in Bed II, the same rocks that were popular during Bed I times continued to be used, but three new types of lava appear among the tools. These are a phonolite, a fine-grained green lava that comes from a small volcano called Engelosen, about five kilometres north of the gorge, and a trachyte (a coarser-grained lava). The trachyte can be seen today in the form of huge blocks at the edge of the Olbalbal Depression opposite Olmoti volcano. They seem to have been deposited here after being carried down on mud-flows from Olmoti, long after the volcano ceased to be active and before the Olbalbal fault trough was formed.

The Engelosen phonolite was a greatly prized material. A few pieces have been found at sites in the lower part of Bed II, but it did not come into common use until Bed IV times, when, at certain sites, it was used to the exclusion of all other rocks. Of the materials used by early man at Olduvai for making stone tools, apart from chert, the phonolite produced the sharpest edges; freshly-struck flakes are nearly as sharp as those of chert or flint.

A very old metamorphic rock called gneiss, which is laminated in structure, occurs at Kelogi inselberg, about nine kilometres south-west of the junction of the two gorges. It is found at sites throughout the Olduvai sequence, from Bed I to the Masek Beds. It is coarse-grained and therefore unsuitable for making sharp cutting and chopping tools, but was widely used for anvils and spheroids. Its preferential use for these two tool-categories suggests that it was perhaps tougher and less liable to shatter under the impact of blows than other rocks that were available.

It will be seen from the map on pp. 52-3 that the sources of the rocks most favoured for making tools were usually at considerable distances from the living sites. Outstanding among these is the green phonolite from Engelosen, which was carried to numerous sites in Bed IV times, sometimes as much as twenty kilometres in direct distance from the source. When the topography of the country is taken into account, the distance travelled on foot must have been much greater. The Olmoti trachyte was also transported to many sites in both Bed II and Bed IV times; it occurs frequently at sites in the side gorge about fifteen kilometres from the nearest known source. The Kelogi gneiss is also found as far as DK, thirteen kilometres to the east. Such transportation of different rocks suggests the possibility that other materials besides the Kelogi gneiss had particular properties and were required for specific uses. It seems likely that there was some form of exchange or barter of rocks among the groups of hominids living in the areas where they occurred, rather than transportation over the entire distance by members of a single group. Trade in various stones for making tools became well-established during the later phases of the Stone Age and it is quite possible that it had already come into being during the Lower and Middle Pleistocene.

For many years it was believed that there was a simple evolutionary sequence of Stone Age cultures, each leading to the next in chronological order, with a steadily progressive improvement in techniques of manufacture. This concept is now known to be false, but there is still a measure of disagreement regarding the early Pleistocene stone industries. Few experts now would dispute that two distinct traditions of tool-making existed: a chopper-small-tool complex and a handaxe-cleaver complex (the Acheulean). These two traditions existed contemporaneously in Africa, but in Europe the chopper-small-tool industries seem to precede the Acheulean – which, in any case, does not extend back into the Lower Pleistocene as it does in Africa.

The chopper-small-tool complex is known as the Oldowan and Developed Oldowan in East Africa and is represented in Europe by the Clactonian (named after the seaside resort in England where it was first found) and the Tayacian (named after the village of Tayac in the Dordogne, France). The principal elements in these industries are small flake tools and choppers. There are some European workers who regard the latter as merely cores or nuclei from which the flakes needed to make the small tools were detached, but in my opinion they are the equivalent of the Oldowan and Developed Oldowan choppers.

The Acheulean or handaxe culture was named after the town of St Acheul in northern France, where handaxes were recognized as human artefacts during the last century. The earlier stages of the Acheulean were formerly termed Chellean, after another town in France, but it is now considered unjustifiable, especially in Africa, to subdivide the handaxe culture; what would formerly have been termed Chellean is now referred to as the lower or early Acheulean.

Opinion is divided as to the reason for the chopper-small-tool and Acheulean industrial traditions being different. One school of thought considers that diverse occupations by the same ethnic groups may have been responsible; for instance, the people of one group were engaged in hunting, while the other was employed in a totally different fashion, perhaps purely in domestic activities. Another view is that diverse ecological conditions might be responsible. A third explanation is that two distinct hominid lineages may have been living contemporaneously. There is little evidence, at present, to indicate which interpretation may be correct, although Richard Hay has observed that at Olduvai during Bed II times the Developed Oldowan sites tend to be nearer to the lake shore than the Acheulean.

To make a tool – whether large or small – it is necessary to remove flakes and chips. Flaking can be carried out by percussion, with a pointed hammerstone, or by means of a cylindrical hammer – for example, the shaft of a long bone; by pressure; or, in the crudest manner, by battering the piece of stone to be flaked against another stone serving as an anvil. The early stone industries are distinguished from one another by the different methods of tool-making, by the size of the flakes removed, and by the types and variety of tools produced.

The Oldowan industry, named after Olduvai Gorge, was first described in the volume published in 1951*. It has a distinctive tool-kit that may differ slightly between one site and another, but which remains the same in its essential elements. 'Pebble tools' or choppers were for a long time considered to be its characteristic tools. Choppers are certainly the most common tools found at Olduvai, and in the days before detailed excavation they were collected and the other small tools generally overlooked.

It is difficult at present to find an exact parallel for the Oldowan industry outside East Africa, although some must surely exist. Choppers are certainly known from early deposits, particularly from several sites in North Africa, but the stratigraphic evidence is poor and associated tools are not recorded so that it is not possible to determine to which industry these choppers may belong.

The water-worn stones, either large pebbles or small

* *Olduvai Gorge: a report on the evolution of the handaxe culture in Beds I-IV*, by L. S. B. Leakey, C.U.P., 1951.

cobbles, on which many of the choppers are made are essentially of a convenient size to hold in the hand. The working edges have been crudely flaked to a sharp, jagged cutting edge and the natural, rounded surface forms the butt. Some choppers are also made on cuboid blocks, but it seems that when a rounded, water-worn stone was available it was preferred, and would certainly be more comfortable to hold. The older term 'pebble tool' has now been generally dropped in favour of chopper or chopping tool.

In 1960 we carried out some experiments with Oldowan-type tools, since the potential usefulness of choppers and other tools found in the Oldowan was very little understood. We acquired the leg of a cow, which Louis skinned, disjointed and cut up with choppers and other tools he had made himself. He found that freshly made, unweathered choppers were adequate tools for cutting through the skin and meat, even if the cuts were somewhat ragged. But choppers were useless for disjointing the leg and cutting through the ligaments that held the bones together, since the edges were too thick. Small quartzite flakes, however, were found to be most serviceable for this purpose and by using them it was not difficult to detach the head of the femur from its socket in the pelvis. Battering the bones to break them open and extract the marrow was most easily carried out by placing the shaft on a stone and hitting it with another, either a chopper or an unworked cobble. The types of fracture that resulted were similar to those often seen on the bones from prehistoric living sites.

It was believed at one time that a 'pebble culture' existed in Uganda that was considerably older than the Oldowan from Olduvai. It was discovered in 1919 by the late E. J. Wayland, then Director of the Uganda Geological Survey; he named it the Kafuan after the Kafu River, where it was found in terrace gravels above the present river bed. The 'choppers' usually consisted of quartzite pebbles, generally rather flat, from which flakes had been detached along one edge, often from one direction only. It has since been shown that the flaking in these stones that simulates human workmanship is one of natural origin, probably caused by percussion in the gravels.

Many years ago a similar 'industry' was found in England by an enthusiastic amateur archaeologist, J. Reid Moir. He called it the Darmsdenian, after Darmsden in Suffolk. The conditions that gave rise to these pseudo-tools seem to have been similar to those that caused the flaking on the pebbles in the Kafu Valley. There were many thousands of pebbles with 'flaking' along one edge and from one direction only. In this case earth pressure may have been responsible.

Stone choppers are still being made by certain primitive peoples. The Turkana tribesmen in the remote north-eastern areas of Kenya make them for rough work. A tribe in South West Africa, discovered by an expedition from the Windhoek Museum, also makes choppers, as well as a variety of stone flake tools. These instances of naturally flaked and present-day choppers are mentioned to emphasize the fact that the presence of choppers in a stone industry is not necessarily significant, nor indicative that the industry is either Oldowan or of an early date.

Industries typical of the Oldowan have been recovered from eleven different sites or levels in the gorge; nine are in Bed I, one at the very base of Bed II and one in the lower part of middle Bed II at a horizon where the Developed Oldowan occurs elsewhere. Enough tools have been found in each case to be certain that the industry is Oldowan. Other sites in Bed I have yielded tools that are also probably Oldowan, but the numbers have been too small to be representative.

Although there is no significant difference between the

industries from the eleven Oldowan occurrences, it is true that the proportionate numbers of the various tool types are not always the same. In general, choppers and other heavy duty tools are more common than light duty tools, such as small scrapers, but this is not always the case. For example, at FLK on the '*Zinjanthropus*' floor, light duty scrapers are more common than any other tool category.

The industry associated with the stone circle at DK, in lower Bed I, is the earliest from which there is a good representative series of tools (see glossary on pp. 110–22 for descriptions of the various tool types). In a total of just under 1200 artefacts, of which 154 are tools, choppers are the most common and amount to 30% of the total, with side choppers outnumbering any other type. Polyhedrons and discoids also occur. The small tools consist of scrapers and burins; there are no awls, laterally trimmed flakes or *outils écaillés*. Symmetrical spheroids are likewise absent here, but there are a few rather crude sub-spheroids. Hammerstones are relatively common and there are a few anvils consisting of large, broken lava cobbles or small boulders, on which the edges of the fractured surface show the battered type of utilization typical of these tools.

The choppers, polyhedrons and discoids are smaller than those from higher levels in Bed I. They compare with some of the tools made on chert nodules from the lower part of Bed II, where, however, the size was clearly controlled by the smallness of the chert nodules employed.

At DK, lava of various sorts was the most common material, not only for the heavy duty tools, for which it was generally preferred throughout the Oldowan, but also for the light duty tools, utilized flakes and *débitage*, which at other sites are mostly of quartzite. The lavas employed are generally the nephelinite from Sadiman and the trachyandesite and basalt from Lemagrut. It is possible that the stream beds containing these rocks were more accessible at this time than the quartzite from the Naibor Soit inselberg, which was later widely used as raw material.

At FLK NN, where the remains of *Homo habilis* were found in 1960, the number of tools is too small for analysis. Nevertheless, those that did occur on the living floor with the hominid remains appear to be entirely typical of the Oldowan.

The occupation floor at FLK, in middle Bed I, on which the remains of *Homo habilis* as well as the skull of *Australopithecus boisei* were found, yielded a total of 2470 artefacts. They included an unusually high percentage of *débitage* and only sixty tools. Quartzite from Naibor Soit is the most common material in all the tool categories, including the choppers, polyhedrons and discoids. Small tools, particularly small scrapers, are more abundant here than at any other Oldowan site.

Artefacts from the six levels that were excavated at FLK North at the top of Bed I are clearly Oldowan. At the elephant kill, 123 artefacts were grouped round the skeleton. Nearly all of them were of quartzite. Five were tools (four choppers and one proto-biface) and the balance utilized material, including six anvils – an unusually high proportion in relation to the number of other types of artefacts. Any interpretation of the purposes for which the tools in this little group may have been used is necessarily guesswork; but one may assume that the choppers and proto-bifaces perhaps served for tearing through the belly-skin of the animal, while the small, sharp flakes may have been used as knives for cutting up the flesh. None of the bones had been broken open and it is difficult to suggest how the anvils were used in connection with butchering the carcass, unless they were for striking fresh flakes as required.

The most prolific horizon at this site lay immediately

beneath the marker Tuff IF and yielded just over 1200 artefacts. An outstanding feature in this assemblage is the skill displayed in the manufacture of choppers, which are more boldly and surely flaked than at any other site. They also greatly outnumber any other tool category and are proportionately twice as common as at DK. Side and end choppers are, as usual, the most abundant types and other varieties are relatively scarce. The majority of choppers and other heavy duty tools is made from lava. Well-made stone balls or spheroids appear for the first time at this level, although they are rare and only three were found. Light duty tools are equally scarce and are only represented by a few small scrapers.

The last Oldowan site to be described is at MNK, in the side gorge, where the skull of OH13 was found: it is in the lower part of middle Bed II. The artefacts were at the same level as two *in situ* fragments of the skull. Forty-five were tools, of which more than half were choppers. In common with the industries from the high levels in Bed I and the base of Bed II, light duty tools were scarce and consisted of only four small scrapers.

At other sites contemporary with the Oldowan at MNK, the industries are Developed Oldowan, in which small tools are not only plentiful but also include a variety of types. It seems, therefore, that for some reason not understood, the makers of the industry at MNK persisted in the Oldowan tradition and did not adopt the enlarged tool-kit that came into use elsewhere at this time.

No shaped bone tools are known from the Oldowan, although they occur at Developed Oldowan sites; but there is one equid rib from FLK NN that shows abrasion at one end, as well as a bovid cannon bone and a limb bone splinter from FLK North whose pointed ends are worn smooth.

The discovery of a lava cobble at FLK North which has

been pecked over the greater part of the surface and also bears a groove that is clearly artificial is wholly unexpected in an Oldowan context. The stone is oblong, measuring $79 \times 54 \times 49$ millimetres, the base and one side being flat, while the upper surface and one side are convex. One end is rather more pointed than the other. The groove encircles the upper, convex surface and measures from 9 to 18 millimetres in width and from 2 to 4.5 millimetres in depth. It is sufficiently deep to hold a thong or cord in position if it is tied round the stone at this point. Although the interior of the groove is smoother than the pecked surface, it shows no trace of wear. In addition to the overall pecking of the surface, there is a line of four symmetrical indentations, 3 to 4 millimetres in diameter and 0.5 millimetres deep, on the convex side, as well as two slightly larger hollows.

Although no explanation of this curious stone can be suggested, it seems unlikely to have served any utilitarian purpose. With imagination it is possible to read an anthropomorphic image into the various peck marks and the grooves: two eyes, an elongated muzzle and the base of the hair line marked by the groove. This suggestion is likely to be quite erroneous, but whatever the true explanation may be, the existence of an apparently non-utility carved stone at this remote period is of great interest.

To sum up: now that complete assemblages of artefacts are known, the Oldowan industry can be shown to include small tools and several types of heavy duty tools as well as choppers, although choppers are by far the most abundant tools and amount to just over half the total number from all the excavated sites.

At Olduvai, the Oldowan of Bed I is followed by the

Broken animal bones and stone tools on a camp site in Bed I

Tusks of *Deinotherium* wrapped in plaster of Paris bandages, ready for removal

One of the hominid footprints found at Laetoli in 1978, dated at 3.6 million years old.

Developed Oldowan, an industry in which there is a more diverse tool-kit as well as a low percentage of bifacial tools (trimmed on both faces). In Beds II, III and IV it is contemporary with the Acheulean industry. The poorly-made handaxes found at Developed Oldowan sites indicate that the makers had not yet acquired the technique of removing large flakes, which is characteristic of the Acheulean industry. The Developed Oldowan tool-kit, however, includes a greater variety of small tools than the Acheulean.

The Developed Oldowan appears to be a local evolution from the Oldowan. It is found throughout middle and upper Bed II and is also present in Bed III and in upper Bed IV. The earliest phase of the industry, found in lower Bed II, still has proto-bifaces, but no true handaxes. In order to distinguish it from the subsequent phase that contains some handaxes, it has been termed Developed Oldowan A; the later phase with some small handaxes, the Developed Oldowan B; and the final phase, in which pitted anvils and hammerstones are abundant, the Developed Oldowan C.

Artefacts belonging to the Developed Oldowan A have been excavated from two different levels at HWK East, where they occur both above and below the Lemuta Member, as well as from one level at FLK North. Choppers, polyhedrons, discoids and heavy duty scrapers are less common in this industry than in the Oldowan, but the numbers of spheroids, sub-spheroids and proto-bifaces have greatly increased. Awls and laterally-trimmed flakes are found for the first time, but there are no burins.

Chert was a favourite material for making small tools and virtually replaced quartzite for this purpose. As we have seen, small choppers and polyhedrons were also made from chert, but owing to the irregularities of the chert nodules they are less symmetrical than those made from lava or quartzite. Even small flakes of chert show evidence of use or trimming, and it seems that this material was used down to the last possible fragment.

Developed Oldowan B industries have been found at three different sites or levels in middle and upper Bed II, namely at SHK in middle Bed II, at BK and on the upper occupation floor at TK in upper Bed II. Two Developed Oldowan C sites are known in upper Bed IV.

In the industry from SHK spheroids and sub-spheroids are the most common tools. There are also light and heavy duty scrapers, polyhedrons and discoids, as well as a few burins and awls.

As we have seen, the industries recovered from the two occupation floors at TK differ from one another in certain respects, particularly in the bifaces. The upper industry appears to be Developed Oldowan and the lower probably Acheulean. The living floors were found on two well-defined palaeosols or ancient land-surfaces, separated by about one metre of deposits. The tools from both levels include burins, awls and laterally trimmed flakes, in addition to small scrapers and the usual heavy duty tools, such as choppers, polyhedrons, discoids and scrapers. *Outils écaillés*, however, occurred only on the lower floor. The handaxes from the lower floor are slightly more numerous than those from the upper floor. They are also large and generally made on slabs of white quartzite, while those from the upper floor are small, crude and mostly made from lava. They strongly resemble the small Developed Oldowan handaxes from BK and SHK, while those from the lower floor are Acheulean in character.

The site at BK consists of a channel cut into the marker Tuff IID. Excavations were carried out there over a number of years prior to the 1960–3 season and yielded a rich fauna as well as over 11,000 artefacts. In the total number of

tools from all the excavations at this site handaxes amount
to 5%. There is also one poorly-made cleaver. The handaxes
are generally small and crude and do not show the technical
skill of the handaxes from the lower floor at TK. The
choppers amount to 14% of the tools. There is a noticeable
difference between this series and the choppers from earlier
levels. They are mostly made from quartzite blocks and not
water-worn stones. The working edges are flaked not only
along the main edge, but also in part round either end. This
makes a longer working edge in relation to the circumference
of the tools than is generally found in choppers made on
lava cobbles. Awls and *outils écaillés* are more numerous
than at any other Developed Oldowan B site.

The latest known manifestation of the Developed Oldowan
is in upper Bed IV. It was recovered from three separate
trenches within a short distance of one another at WK East
and PDK. Since all three trenches were located within the
same rather wide river channel and were at the same stratigraphic level, the tools have been pooled for study.

A noticeable feature of this industry, in which 725 tools
were found, is the total absence of cleavers and the low
percentage of small, poorly-made handaxes. Various small
tools, generally made of quartzite, are particularly abundant;
small scrapers alone amount to nearly half the total and some
are microlithic in size. Other small tools include *outils
écaillés*, punches, burins, awls and a few small laterally
trimmed flakes. Choppers, spheroids and discoids are
scarce, whilst the 'handaxes' amount to only 13%. They do
not resemble the handaxes known from any other site in
Bed IV, but stand very close to those from BK, the upper
floor at TK and SHK. They are not only small, but often
markedly asymmetrical and crudely flaked, with frequent
step-flaking. Quartzite punches, small rod-like tools,
amount to 20% of the total and are often double-ended,

showing crushing at either end. Pitted anvils and hammerstones are abundant.

To sum up: eleven types of tools can be recognized from the Developed Oldowan B localities that were excavated. They consist of bifaces, choppers, polyhedrons, discoids, spheroids and sub-spheroids, heavy and light duty scrapers, burins, awls, *outils écaillés* and laterally trimmed flakes. Spheroids and sub-spheroids are the most common tools. An analysis of weight shows that the really massive specimens weighing several kilograms, which are found in middle Bed II, do not occur either in lower or upper Bed II. In upper Bed II, also, a larger proportion weigh under 500 grams than in the earlier levels. If these tools were, in fact, missiles, and used as bolas, as has been suggested, this reduction in general size may reflect some change in the way they were used or in the type of game hunted.

Choppers are the next most common tool in the industry, followed by a variety of light duty scrapers. Although not common, awls are fairly well represented. Burins are always made from quartzite, with angle burins predominating. The *outils écaillés*, also made from quartzite, are both single and double ended.

Whereas no appreciable changes can be seen between the early and later occurrences of the Oldowan from lower Bed I to the base of Bed II, noticeable differences are evident in the Developed Oldowan A, B and C from lower and upper Bed II and upper Bed IV. These lie essentially in an expansion of the industry brought about by the introduction of new tool types, for example, punches, pitted anvils and hammerstones, which are among the principal tools of Developed Oldowan C.

As has been seen, the geological evidence indicates that the deposits of Bed II represent a much longer period (about 600,000 years) than those of Bed I. During such time considerable changes could be expected in any industry even without external stimulus. In the Developed Oldowan two factors may have served as stimuli and contributed to its expansion: first, the availability of chert, which almost certainly stimulated the manufacture of small tools; and second, the occurrence of the Acheulean in middle Bed II from which the concept of bifacial tools may have been derived.

The Acheulean is a cultural complex in which large tools flaked on both faces, known as handaxes and cleavers, are predominant (these are also sometimes referred to as bifaces and as bifacial tools). Handaxes are generally oval in shape, with a pointed tip and rounded butt; cleavers have a wide, transverse adze-like cutting edge. The Acheulean is found throughout Africa, in Europe and in parts of Asia, and it is probably the most widespread and long-lasting of all prehistoric traditions in tool-making. We do not know whether its distribution is due to independent invention, the rapid adoption of a new idea by various prehistoric peoples, or to the inventors – perhaps *Homo erectus* – spreading a new fashion in tools as they migrated.

We have not yet found the beginning of the Acheulean, although the early Acheulean from Bed II at Olduvai, which probably dates to about 1,400,000 years, is among the earliest known. A terminal date for the Acheulean is uncertain, but evidence from a number of sites in Africa suggest that it may have come to an end about 200,000 years ago.

In Africa the whole handaxe/cleaver complex is now known as Acheulean. The character that used to be considered critical for separating the Acheulean from the 'Chellean' was the presence of shallow, rather flat trimming scars, referred to either as 'wood technique' or 'cylinder hammer technique', in which the flakes were probably removed by means of a cylindrical instrument so that the force was fairly widely distributed. The 'Chellean' type of trimming scars are deep, with pronounced intervening ridges, and the flakes were detached by means of a pointed hammerstone.

It is true that the shallow type of flaking is found in the later Acheulean and not, for example, in the early Acheulean of Bed II; but it is equally true that assemblages of handaxes made by means of the deeply indented 'Chellean' type of flaking are contemporaneous and even post-date others characterized by the shallow, 'cylinder hammer' type of flaking. The importance of the type of flaking shown by any group of handaxes and/or cleavers, therefore, must not be over-emphasized, and cannot be used as a criterion of age, as it was in the past. It is now known to depend largely on the nature of the raw materials which required a number of different techniques to achieve the best results. In spite of the number of years during which handaxes have been known and studied, it is still by no means certain which characters can be relied on to distinguish one Acheulean group from another. It is equally uncertain whether the differences we see are really significant in a far-reaching sense, or merely reflect local trends, such as fashions preferred by family or tribal groups.

Unfortunately prehistorians have no evidence as to how either handaxes or cleavers were used. The term handaxe is perhaps a misnomer, since if these sharp-edged tools are held in the hand when they are used for cutting, chopping or digging, they are liable to cut into the palm. It seems more likely that they were hafted; but if so, it is strange that the cutting edge normally extends round the entire circumference and has also frequently been chipped by use along its whole length. Cleavers are thought to have been skinning and flaying tools, but there is no real evidence to support this assumption.

Handaxes were the first stone tools to be recognized in England and France as implements of bygone man. I am proud to say that one of my direct ancestors, John Frere of Hoxne in Suffolk, was the first to state unequivocally that handaxes were man-made. They had been noticed previously and had aroused curiosity, but were generally thought to be thunderbolts or other freaks of nature.

In a letter to the Secretary of the Society of Antiquaries, read on 22 June 1797, John Frere wrote as follows:

Sir,

I take the liberty to request you to lay before the Society some flints found in the parish of Hoxne, in the county of Suffolk, which, if not particularly objects of curiosity themselves, must, I think, be considered in that light, from the situation in which they were found.

They are, I think, evidently weapons of war, fabricated and used by a people who had not the use of metals. They lay in great numbers at the depth of about twelve feet, in a stratified soil, which was dug into for the purpose of raising clay for bricks.

After listing the various strata and remarking that some bones had also been found, particularly a 'jaw bone of enormous size, of some unknown animal', John Frere's letter continued:

The situation in which these weapons were found may tempt us to refer them to a very remote period indeed; even beyond that of the present world, but, whatever our conjectures on that head may be, it will be difficult to account for the stratum in which they lie being covered by another stratum, which, on that supposition, may be conjectured to have been once the bottom, or at least the shore of the sea. The manner in which they lie would lead to the persuasion that it was a place of their manufacture and not of their accidental deposit; and the numbers of them were so great that the man who carried on the brick-work told me that, before he was aware of their being objects of curiosity, he had emptied baskets of them into the ruts of an adjoining road.

John Frere's recognition of handaxes as humanly fashioned tools was followed by Boucher de Perthes in France, who, in 1846, also stated his conviction that they were artefacts.

Handaxes, if they are well-made, are probably among the most aesthetically pleasing tools made by prehistoric man – excluding the polished stone implements of much later times. This had disastrous consequences for the Acheulean sites in Europe. Both professional and amateur archaeologists, members of field clubs and natural history societies one and all collected handaxes over the years, with almost total disregard for the geological context, associated artefacts or fauna. There were, of course, some notable exceptions to whom we owe a debt of gratitude. But even as late as the 1930s collectors were still visiting the commercial gravel pits in England and France and bribing the workmen to save handaxes for them.

Small tools were for a long time disregarded in the Acheulean. Today, although all the artefacts from Acheulean sites are saved and eventually analysed, there is still no clear picture of the small-tool kit that normally accompanies handaxes and cleavers in Europe.

At Olduvai, EF-HR is the only early Acheulean site yet excavated. It lies a few feet above the Lemuta Member and appears to have been a small camping place beside a shallow stream. Just over four hundred artefacts were recovered, of which ninety-one are tools. Of these, the large bifacial tools amount to over half the total. They consist of forty-eight handaxes and one cleaver, a proportion that leaves no doubt that this is an Acheulean industry.

With few exceptions, the handaxes as well as the single cleaver are made on large lava flakes. Many retain areas of rounded weathered surface on the upper face, indicating that the flakes were struck from boulders. Usually, the main flake surface has remained almost unretouched, with only a few flakes removed in order to trim off the striking platform and the bulb of percussion. The handaxes are generally pointed, but there is great variation in shape. Only a limited number of other tools were found in association; they consist of a few choppers, polyhedrons, discoids, spheroids and scrapers.

So far, only a preliminary survey of the industries from Bed IV and the Masek Beds has been carried out. This has been confined to a record of the tool categories in each assemblage, the average size of the handaxes and cleavers and the average number of trimming scars that they show. It is evident, even on the basis of this preliminary analysis, that there is considerable variation between the tool-kits from the different sites and levels, both in their components and in the character of the handaxes and cleavers. This applies not only to those from different levels, but also to those that are broadly contemporaneous and situated close to one another geographically. The tools within each 'unit', however, conform closely in size and technique of manufacture.

It will be remembered that there are three marker horizons in Bed IV, Tuff IVA (the lowest), one or more grey siltstones and Tuff IVB, which is above the siltstones. Unfortunately, the extensive channelling that took place during Bed IV has often cut out these marker beds, so that they are not always present in critical areas. At HEB, however, all the tool-bearing levels are beneath one of the grey siltstones, whilst at WK and other sites in the same area they are not only above a grey siltstone, but also more recent than Tuff IVB.

The industries from HEB will be considered first, since they are the earliest group. It has been shown that the lowest level with artefacts is within a small stream channel. In this industry the handaxes occur in almost equal proportions to the choppers, spheroids and small scrapers; other small tools are rare.

A second level of artefacts and fossil bones at HEB was found by the late Dr J. Waechter in 1962; it is approximately thirty centimetres higher than the channel. The handaxes and cleavers greatly outnumber any other tool category and amount to more than half the total. They are mostly made from the Engelosen phonolite and are elaborately trimmed, with numerous flat trimming scars. Although the tools have been made on flakes, both faces have generally been so thoroughly trimmed that only a few specimens retain part of the original flake surface.

The third artefact-bearing level at this site consists of a river sand that contained dense concentrations of tools in certain areas. Handaxes and cleavers are again the most common types of tools and account for half the total. They are mostly made on flakes struck from boulders of trachyandesite, with the original flake surface only partially trimmed away. On the whole, they are slightly larger than those from either of the earlier levels. A fourth level containing artefacts occurs at the western end of the site, about thirty centimetres higher. The handaxes and cleavers from this level are very similar to those from the third level.

In the WK East and PDK group of sites, about two kilometres down the main gorge from HEB, a level containing artefacts was found at the junction of Beds III and IV. The tools were on an uneven surface and some were lying on edge, but their positions appeared to be due to the irregularity of the underlying surface rather than to human agency. This level yielded only thirty-eight tools, but handaxes and cleavers are relatively common and amount to half the total. They are considerably larger than those from the higher levels in this area. The cleavers include 'waisted' examples with a constriction below the cutting edge, which is consequently flared outwards on either side. The relationship of this horizon to the lowest level at HEB is uncertain, but it may possibly be earlier.

The site WK is just under one kilometre to the west of PDK. It consists of a channel cut through Tuff IVB, blocks of which can be seen in the channel filling. A grey siltstone, similar to that which overlies the artefact levels at HEB, occurs here half to one metre below the tool-bearing horizon. The artefacts, as well as fossil bones and large numbers of cobbles and pebbles, were concentrated within the channel and other depressions on the occupation surface, while the two bones of *Homo erectus* were on the higher ground alongside the channel.

In the WK industry cleavers and handaxes are the most common tool categories, amounting to about one third of the total. Both cleavers and handaxes have been made on large flakes, struck from lava boulders, in which the original flake surface has been only partially trimmed away. This has resulted in a very low number of trimming scars – as low, in fact, as that for the early Acheulean of Bed II, to which the industry from WK bears a strong resemblance. Discoids, spheroids and scrapers also occur, but the most numerous tools, following the handaxes and cleavers, are pitted anvils and hammerstones, which amount to a quarter of the total.

We have seen that the only site known in the Masek Beds is at FLK, in the cliff that overlooks the main FLK site in

Bed I. Although the handaxes and other artefacts were in a sandy river deposit within a shallow channel, they are in exceptionally sharp condition. This is all the more remarkable since most of the handaxes are made from white quartzite and have been trimmed with great refinement to thin, tapering points and fine, even cutting edges all round the circumference. In a material as brittle as quartzite, transportation in the stream bed, even for a short distance, could be expected to cause some visible damage.

There are no cleavers in this industry, but the handaxes are the largest and probably the most highly finished of any Acheulean industry at Olduvai. Also, five of the largest specimens are so closely comparable in all dimensions, as well as in technique of manufacture, that one can only believe they were the work of one man.

Small scrapers are particularly abundant and amount to nearly half the tools. A proportion are so small that they fall well within the range of microliths and contrast most markedly with the size of the handaxes. Apart from spheroids, which occur in almost equal proportion to the handaxes, heavy duty tools are scarce.

The excavations in Bed IV have demonstrated that there was considerable divergence among the industries that can be attributed to the Acheulean, and that the Developed Oldowan persisted. There is no evidence to suggest that there was any discernible evolutionary advance in the manufacture of the handaxes and cleavers. On the contrary, the occurrence of bifacial tools with deeply indented flake scars, which used to be considered a 'Chellean' characteristic, in upper Bed IV, and of others with elaborate shallow flaking in lower Bed IV, demonstrates that this was not the case. On the basis of the facts now available, the most likely explanation seems to be that there were various local schools or traditions of tool-making in the Acheulean, especially for handaxes and cleavers.

Besides the Developed Oldowan and Acheulean from the sites described above, industries were found at three other sites in middle and upper Bed II that cannot be accommodated in either group. These are from MNK main site, FC West and the lower living floor at TK. In each case the tool components and variety of bifaces suggest affinities with the Developed Oldowan, but the character of the handaxes is wholly Acheulean. They are large, boldly and expertly flaked and show no similarity to the small, poorly-made bifacial tools of the Developed Oldowan. It is probable that further fieldwork will be necessary to determine the cultural relationship of these industries.

The artefacts from the Ndutu and Naisiusiu Beds carry forward the story of prehistoric man at Olduvai to about 17,000 years ago. No living sites are known in the Ndutu Beds but there are a few localities near the mouth of the gorge where scattered tools have been found by Richard Hay and his field assistant Lucas Kioko. They are characteristic of what is known as the middle Stone Age. This was a specialized development in the making of stone tools which was adopted over most parts of the world inhabited by early man, replacing the handaxe culture.

Instead of detaching a flake from its parent block or core and then trimming it into shape, as had been the practice until the advent of this technique, the shaping of the flake took place while it was still on the core. For this reason, it is sometimes spoken of as the 'prepared core technique'. It was first recognized at Levallois, in France, and is also known as the Levallois technique. The cores are oblong or discoidal, trimmed all round the circumference with a striking platform at one end or one side. An unstruck core has a domed upper surface, but when the flake has been removed there is a negative, concave scar. Both struck and unstruck cores have been found in the Ndutu Beds, as well as the flakes struck from them. These are often triangular in shape, with a broad, 'faceted' striking platform, made by the truncation of the preparatory flake scars. Bifacially trimmed points that were probably hafted as spears or lances are often associated with this industry, but none has yet been found at Olduvai.

Flakes and cores of this type are particularly abundant at Laetoli and in the vicinity of Lake Eyasi, to the south of Olduvai, where they can be found on the surface in many places and where they were also associated with parts of the three human skulls. These skulls are very fragmentary but almost certainly belong to the same lineage as Rhodesian Man – the African equivalent of Neanderthal Man, with pronounced brow ridges, but with a brain case similar to *Homo sapiens*. At Laetoli they have also been found with a human skull which is now being studied.

Only one locality with artefacts is known in the Naisiusiu Beds: a living site in the bottom of the gorge near the Second Fault which is exposed in the side of a low hillock formed by the Naisiusiu Beds. There are many artefacts and a level of burned bones, the majority of which belong to zebra. The tools are late Stone Age and include the geometric forms that characterize this period, such as small knife blades with blunted backs and many small scrapers. They are made from both obsidian and chert, with a few of the larger flakes made of quartzite. The source of the obsidian has not yet been located, but the chert is likely to have been obtained from the cliff at MNK.

Although beads made from ostrich eggshell are a common feature at most late Stone Age sites, none was found at the Naisiusiu site. However, there were numerous pieces of ostrich eggshell. They have been used for carbon 14 dating and have given a figure of 17,000 years BP. A second date of 17,000 ± 1000 years BP has been obtained by carbon 14, based on the collagen from the bones. These are probably the earliest dates so far known for a microlithic industry of the late Stone Age.

The human skeleton that was found by Professor Reck in 1913, whose age became the subject of widespread controversy, now appears to be linked with the microlithic site in the Naisiusiu Beds. Dr Reiner Protsch, formerly of the Department of Physics, University of California at Los Angeles, obtained some bones from this skeleton while on a visit to Germany. He has since carried out tests for carbon 14 dating and has obtained the interesting figure of 16,920 ± 920 years BP, which is remarkably close to the dates obtained from the living site.

Still later in the prehistory of the gorge, Neolithic man occupied the area, at least for a while. A particularly fine ground stone axe was found by Louis at the rim of the TK gully some years ago, while pieces of stone bowls, grindstones and pestle-rubbers have also been collected in the past. By analogy with the burial mounds containing stone bowls in Ngorongoro Crater, and with dated stone bowl sites in Kenya, this last phase of Stone Age occupation probably took place between 2600 and 2800 years BP.

It will be helpful to conclude this chapter with a glossary of the principal tools of the Oldowan, Developed Oldowan and Acheulean industries.

Glossary of Tools

Anvils

The anvils found at Olduvai fall into two groups: (a) cuboid or circular blocks, often made of gneiss or tabular quartzite, with flat upper and lower faces and nearly vertical sides and (b) stones with pitted hollows. In the first group, the edges are battered, with many plunging flake scars, while the upper and lower faces also show marks of blows. In Bed I the anvils are usually natural blocks of rock that have not been shaped before use; but in Bed II they have sometimes been roughly shaped. Pitted anvils of the second type are found commonly in Bed IV, although rare examples are known earlier; there is even one specimen from lower Bed II and another from the top of Bed I. They consist of lava cobbles and small boulders on which there are roughly pitted hollows. These hollows occur singly, in pairs, or one on either side of the stone. Occasionally there are multiple hollows: in one six-sided example there are six, one on each face of the stone. The hollows vary in diameter from one to seven centimetres, and the depth is also variable. The interiors are always rough and appear to have been pecked.

It is probable that these anvils may have resulted from the use of the bi-polar technique for detaching flakes. In this method the core from which a flake is to be knocked off is placed on an anvil and hit at the opposite end with a hammer-stone. A second suggestion is that the pitted anvils and small quartzite points described below as punches were used together for punching holes in hides.

Length of figured specimen 8 cm.

Awls

These small, sharp points are trimmed or notched on either side. They are unknown in Bed I and first appear in lower Bed II when chert came into use for making tools. They are most common in upper Bed II. In more recent pre-historic times, such tools have been used for piercing leather.

Length of figured specimen 3·5 cm

Bifacial points

These are generally flakes in which both the upper and lower faces have been trimmed to form a roughly triangular, pointed tool. They are cruder and more asymmetrical than the bifacial points that became common in later industries, but like the proto-bifaces, they appear to represent early, unskilful attempts to make a tool that was later perfected. The later bifacial points are thought to have been used as lance or spear heads and it is possible that even the crude, early examples were put to a similar purpose.

Length of figured specimen 4·5 cm.

Burins or Chisels

Burins are found at nearly all Oldowan and Developed Oldowan sites, but they are always scarce. They are characterized by a short, thick-set working edge, usually set at right angles to the upper and lower faces of the tools. The most common type is known as an angle burin: these are often made on broken flakes in which the transverse fracture has had one or two long, narrow flakes removed from one side to form the working edge (such burin-trimming flakes are known as spalls). Before their discovery in Bed I at Olduvai, burins were considered to be essentially Middle and Upper Pleistocene tools. Finding these tools in Bed I shows that they go back to Lower Pleistocene times.

Length of figured specimen 4·7 cm.

Choppers

These are usually made on water-worn lava cobbles in which the natural, smooth surface of the stone forms a rounded butt that could be comfortably held in the hand. The working edges are sharp, with relatively large flake scars, usually detached alternately from either face to form a jagged edge. The most common type of chopper at Olduvai is a side chopper, in which the working edge is along the side of an oblong stone. There are also end, two-edged, pointed and chisel-edged choppers; these last three categories always being rare.

Length of figured specimen 7·5 cm.

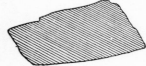

Cleavers

These tools have a broad, transverse, adze-like cutting edge at the tip, either straight or oblique, and come under the general category of bifaces since they are usually trimmed on both faces. They are characteristic of the Acheulean but are more common in Africa than in Europe, probably because the African raw materials were more suitable for making this type of tool than the flint used in Europe. It has been suggested that cleavers were used for skinning, but this is by no means sure.

Length of figured specimen 14·7 cm.

114

Débitage

Large numbers of flakes and other apparent waste material are found which show neither trimming nor wear. At many other sites these can be regarded correctly as waste material discarded while tools were made; but at Olduvai this does not appear to be the case, particularly in Bed I, where the heavy duty tools, such as choppers, polyhedrons and discoids, are mostly made from water-worn cobbles and pebbles of various lavas, while the flakes that show neither trimming nor usage are mostly of quartzite, as are the light duty utilized flakes. The number of lava flakes associated with the big lava tools is too small at all sites (except DK) to represent the waste flakes detached when these tools were made. This situation can only mean that the heavy duty lava tools were not made on the living sites but were made elsewhere, probably wherever the rocks were obtained. The quartzite flakes, therefore, were not waste, but served a purpose of their own. I am inclined to believe that they were expressly made to serve as small, sharp knives. The terms 'waste' and 'debris', therefore, seem to be inapplicable and I have preferred the term *débitage*, since this does not mean only discarded rubbish.

Length of figured specimen 3·5 cm.

Discoids

These are roughly circular with a jagged, sharp edge on the circumference, trimmed all round, on both the upper and lower faces. They are generally flattened, with an elliptical cross-section. In Bed I times they were often made from a broken cobble, so that one face was flat and the opposite markedly convex. Like choppers and polyhedrons, discoids seem to have been used for cutting.

Length of figured specimen 3·7 cm.

Hammerstones

These are of two types. The first consists of water-worn cobbles or pebbles, generally of lava, with battering and bruising of the ends. They were not shaped before use, and were probably used for pounding roots or nuts as well as knocking off flakes. The second group, which has been found in Bed IV, is associated with the pitted anvils. They show similar pits, sometimes in pairs. An experiment by P. R. Jones has shown that this can occur easily when flaking is carried out by the bi-polar technique, particularly when quartzite is flaked.

Length of figured specimen 9 cm.

Handaxes

These are pointed tools, generally with rounded butts and flaked over both faces, with a cutting edge round the whole or most of the circumference. Handaxes have been subdivided into numerous categories according to their form, but it is doubtful whether this classification is of much significance. The term 'handaxe' itself is probably misleading, since it is questionable that these tools were held in the hand and/or hafted. Whether hafted or unhafted, they seem to have been the general utility tool which succeeded the chopper.

Length of figured specimen 10·7 cm.

Laterally Trimmed Flakes

Flakes showing trimming along one or both edges are common in the later Developed Oldowan sites. Some are pointed, but this does not seem to be an essential character. Most are about five centimetres in length and they are not noticeably symmetrical; their use is obscure.

Length of figured specimen 6 cm.

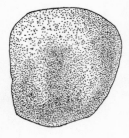

Manuports

Rounded water-worn stones, brought to the sites by man but showing no evidence of either working or use, are a common feature at nearly all the Olduvai sites. They have been termed 'manuports', meaning 'carried by hand'. Their purpose is difficult to explain, but it is possible they were kept handy on the living floors to throw at intruding animals.

Length of figured specimen 7 cm.

Outils Écaillés

No precise English translation of this French term exists, although it means broadly 'scaled tools'. The working edges are wide, straight, or slightly concave, usually blunt, with the appearance of having been crushed. The edges usually extend across the width of the tools with a number of small, flat scars removed on one or both faces. Some examples are double-ended. These tools were formerly considered characteristic of the upper Palaeolithic but have now been found in middle Bed II as well as in the later sites. They do not occur in Bed I. Although *outils écaillés* are classified as tools they may not have been shaped by hand and the type of flaking they show may have resulted from some specialized form of use.

Length of figured specimen 3·8 cm.

Picks

A few massive tools occur in Beds II and IV in which the tips are sharply pointed and the butts large and relatively heavy. None has been found in Bed I.

Length of figured specimen 12 cm.

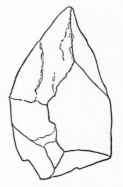

Polyhedrons

These are angular tools, sometimes sub-spherical, with three or more sharp edges, usually intersecting and flaked from either side (the better-made, more symmetrical specimens grade into the less well-made and more irregular sub-spheroids, see below). The use to which polyhedrons were put is uncertain, but the cutting edges appear to have been the principal feature and often show traces of wear.

Length of figured specimen 5·3 cm.

119

Proto Bifaces

These tools are intermediate between choppers and handaxes. They are often made on water-worn stones and are generally partially flaked over both faces (hence the term bifaces), as well as at the tip. The working edges are more jagged than in most handaxes and usually extend round only part of the circumference. The butt ends are generally a natural water-worn surface. No two specimens are alike in method of manufacture. These tools seem to represent the first crude attempts to make a pointed implement with a sharp edge on the circumference, which later developed into handaxes. They represent an advance on side and end choppers, which were generally without points.

Length of figured specimen 14 cm.

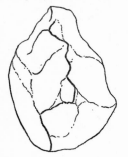

Punches

At sites where the pitted anvils and hammerstones were common, a number of small, thick-set, rod-like fragments of quartzite were found, which may have been used in conjunction with the pitted stones. Both single and double-ended specimens occur, but the former are more common. They are always of quartz or quartzite and are not more than 5 centimetres long and about 1 to 1.5 centimetres in diameter. The tips are crushed and blunted.

Length of figured specimen 4·5 cm.

Scrapers

A variety of different forms of scrapers occurs, including side, end, hollow, discoidal, perimetal and nosed scrapers. Small, light duty specimens are the most common, but there are also heavy duty scrapers, sometimes called push-planes. In most scrapers, the working edges are steeply trimmed from a flat undersurface and the edge of the tool is generally rounded and slightly spoon-shaped. Hollow scrapers were almost certainly used as spoke shaves, for paring down wooden shafts. Small, rounded scrapers and some of the other forms may have been used for working hides.

Length of figured specimen 5 cm.

Spheroids and Sub-spheroids

These include symmetrical stone balls, smoothly finished over the entire surface, as well as faceted examples in which the ridges between the flake scars have been only partly removed or not at all. The use of these tools is uncertain, but it is possible they were missiles used as bolas, two or more being strung together and then hurled at the legs of animals. They first appear in the upper part of Bed I and become increasingly common throughout Bed II. At Olduvai, in Bed IV and at the single site in the Masek Beds, they are rare, although they occur elsewhere in Acheulean sites that are probably contemporary.

Length of figured specimen 4·6 cm.

Utilized Material

In addition to the categories of tools described above, there are usually flakes and other pieces of stone, chipped and blunted along the edges, which have clearly been used for one purpose or another, although they do not conform to any particular type of tool. When describing the stone industries from Beds I and II in my monograph, I have subdivided the utilized material into heavy and light duty – that is, cobbles and blocks and large flakes as opposed to small flakes and other fragments.

Length of figured specimen 6·5 cm.

CHAPTER SEVEN
The Fossil Fauna

STUDY OF THE FOSSIL FAUNA from Olduvai lags behind nearly every other aspect of the research. This is partly due to the scarcity of vertebrate palaeontologists qualified to study the material and partly to the fact that those who could undertake the study are generally committed to university teaching posts and are unable to spend much time on other projects.

The volume of material from Olduvai, particularly in certain groups, has been another factor that has delayed publication. Specialists who are sufficiently interested will find time to describe a few dozen specimens, but when the collections run into thousands the situation is very different. For this reason, it is the groups with most material and, therefore, of the most importance, that are still outstanding, although the specimens have been with the specialists for a number of years. Most notable among these collections are the fossil birds; they are the largest Pleistocene collection in existence.

Some studies of the smaller groups are already published. They include the fish, snakes, elephant shrews, hedgehogs, Muridae (one of the rodent families), carnivores, Equidae (horse family), a chalicothere (a large ungulate with claws), rhinoceroses, hippopotami, giraffes, bovids (antelopes) and gazelles.

For the time being, it is only possible to include here summaries of papers published since Louis wrote volume I of the Olduvai monographs. More detailed notes provided by the authorities who are studying the fauna will be found at the end of this chapter.

The first important fact demonstrated by the fauna of Olduvai is that no true forest-dwellers are present – unless there has been a radical change of habitat in certain animals since Pleistocene times, which seems most improbable. For a while it was believed that okapi occurred in Beds I and II, but the presence of this essentially forest-loving animal appeared such an anomaly that the diagnosis was treated with reserve by myself and others. It has since proved to be erroneous: the remains in question actually belong to the small giraffe also found at Laetoli, East Turkana and elsewhere.

The only other animal that possibly suggests a woodland habitat is the single specimen of a chalicothere (*Ancylotherium hennigi*) found many years ago in lower Bed I. In view of the associated fauna, however, the wooded territory generally linked with chalicotheres seems more likely to have been in the form of gallery forests along rivers than a densely forested terrain.

There is evidence, however, to indicate that the climate of lower Bed I was wetter than in the upper part of the bed. This conclusion is based on the presence of a certain type of slug, a species of elephant shrew and several species of rodents, none of which, it is believed, could have existed under the relatively dry climatic conditions prevailing in the area today. In upper Bed I times, too, the conditions were probably too dry for these species to subsist, since the deposits contain other small mammals such as naked mole rats that are adapted to dry conditions. The rodents and the fossil pollen spectrum both indicate that the climate became wetter again in lower Bed II.

The existence of a permanent lake during Bed I and lower Bed II times, already demonstrated by the geological evidence, is fully confirmed by the fauna, particularly by the fossil birds. These include a wide variety of different families, with many swimmers and waders such as ducks, pelicans, cormorants, grebes and so on, none of which lives in the Olduvai area today. Flamingoes have also been found at a number of sites, indicating that the lake was sufficiently alkaline to contain the rotifers and other micro-organisms that flamingoes live on. The overall picture of the Olduvai avifauna suggests that conditions during Bed I and lower Bed II may have resembled quite closely the present-day environment of East African soda lakes such as Manyara and Natron, where fresh-water streams flow into the soda lakes down the escarpments from the highlands.

The evidence of the fossil fish from Olduvai points to the existence of both alkaline and fresh water in the area. The cichlids are tolerant of water with quite high alkalinity and are even found in parts of Lake Magadi, a soda lake in which the deposits of soda are exploited commercially. Clariidae, which include catfish, require fresh water, although the extent to which they will tolerate brackish water does not appear to be recorded. At FLK North, in upper Bed I, only cichlids were found, indicating that the site was near the lake, but probably not close to any fresh water, in view of the absence of catfish. The existence of a permanent body of water at this site is confirmed by the fossil frogs, all of which belong to families requiring access to permanent water.

On the basis of present-day parallels, the living sites in Beds I and II that contain both cichlids and Clariidae are likely to have been situated near the lake, in places where there were also fresh-water streams – an environment also indicated by the geological evidence.

The fact that Clariidae outnumber cichlids at most living sites is most likely due to the fact that these sluggish fish can be speared or even caught by hand quite easily, whereas cichlids would be difficult to catch in any quantity without traps or nets.

Although the birds, larger mammals and terrestrial reptiles probably moved freely throughout East Africa in prehistoric times, the fossil remains of crocodiles and hippopotami indicate that local populations of these two aquatic groups became cut off in early times and evolved independently within their own areas, becoming more specialized as time went on. The distribution of the crocodiles has many puzzling features. Why are there no representatives of tomistomids at Olduvai, such as *Euthecodon* (a long-snouted, fish-eating crocodile, resembling the gavials), when this family has living representatives? Why, too, is *Crocodilus catafractus* absent at Olduvai, which is geographically close to its present habitat in central Africa, whilst it is found in the distant Turkana basin? Again, why did the broad-snouted, unnamed species that is present at Olduvai as well as at East Turkana and in the Omo Valley leave no living representatives? It is all the more inexplicable since this crocodile shows no over-specialization and also persisted into Middle Pleistocene times elsewhere.

It is possible that *Crocodilus catafractus* reached the Turkana basin by way of the western Rift, by-passing the Olduvai area, or alternatively, that it went south from Turkana by the same route. The fact that *Euthecodon* never came as far south as Olduvai, not even as far as the Baringo basin, may be due to the fact that it originated in the north, where it is known in the Miocene of Egypt.

The tendency in hippopotami for the eye sockets to become

elevated and the muzzles to become longer and flatter is evident in all the different lineages, from Olduvai, East Turkana and the Omo Valley. At Olduvai, however, this specialization went further than elsewhere and in a skull of *Hippopotamus gorgops* from Bed IV it was carried to the extreme. As in the case of the crocodiles, the same species are not present at all three localities. The small hippo with six incisor teeth that is common at East Turkana and at the Omo does not occur at Olduvai. Conversely, the pigmy hippo with four incisors (unnamed) that is found in upper Bed II at Olduvai is not known in the Turkana basin.

Primates are poorly represented at Olduvai. Apart from the single skull of an unusual colobine monkey and a few teeth suggesting a mangabey, there is no evidence of arboreal monkeys. The extinct baboon *Theropithecus oswaldi* (formerly known as *Simopithecus*) is the only primate apart from hominids to occur in any quantity, but it has never been found in such concentrations as at the Acheulean site of Olorgesailie in Kenya, where it clearly formed the principal article of diet at one of the living sites.

The giraffids now seem to fall into two species, *G. jumae* and a pigmy species, *G. stillei*, as well as *Sivatherium*, also present at Laetoli, East Turkana and the Omo. Whether the species are identical in the different areas will only be known when further material becomes available, but it is unlikely that they are far removed from one another.

Among the Bovidae, there are considerable differences between the genera and species found at Olduvai and those from the Turkana basin. The latter are still under study, but many of the discrepancies can probably be explained by difference in time and ecological conditions. The Olduvai Bovidae are mostly ancestral to the living animals, although some extinct species occur. The gazelles, however, are closer to the South African springbok than they are to the present-day East African Grant's and Thomson's gazelles. The Middle Pleistocene giantism that is evident in the pigs and in *Theropithecus* is also evident in the Bovidae. *Pelorovis oldowayensis*, with a horn span of two metres, is a well-known example.

Notes on the Molluscs, Fish, Reptiles, Birds and Mammals found at Olduvai

I am deeply grateful to those authorities who have provided me with information in advance of their own publications.

MOLLUSCS

Molluscs and land snails are poorly represented. A few bivalves have been found in Beds III and IV. Some were complete, with both sides intact, and clearly had not been broken open and eaten by early man. A type of slug, belonging to the family Uricyclidae, which has a small bony plate on its back, occurs quite often in lower Bed I, at DK and FLK NN, and more rarely at FLK, in middle Bed I. The living representatives of these slugs are common only where rainfall exceeds 110 centimetres per year, or where damp conditions are maintained by permanent mist.

Three species of gasteropods (snails) have been found in lower Bed II, but are not of ecological significance since their living representatives are widely distributed in various habitats. Broken shells of a large land snail, similar to *Acha-*

tina in size, have also been found in the lower part of middle Bed II at the MNK skull site, where OH13 was discovered; these snails may have been eaten by early man.

The upper Ndutu Beds have yielded both *Achatina* and *Limicolaria* while the latter also occurs in the Masek Beds. Specific identifications have not been possible, but living forms of both these snails occur at Olduvai today and indicate a relatively dry climate.

FISH

Dr Humphrey Greenwood of the British Museum of Natural History has studied the fossil fish from Beds I and II. With the possible exception of a single bone from FLK, all the specimens have been identified as belonging to two families, the Clariidae, which include catfish, and the Cichlidae, which include *Tilapia*. Since Dr Greenwood's conclusions bear on the environmental conditions during the time of Beds I and II, the final section of his report is quoted in full:

In every deposit where both families are represented the clariid remains outnumber those of the cichlids (as do the number of individual clariids). Because the skeleton of a clariid fish is more robust than a cichlid and also because it contains a greater number of certain elements (e.g. vertebrae and fin rays) the magnitude of these differences must be treated with caution. Nevertheless, it seems that clariids were the more abundant fishes.

It is difficult to interpret the significance of there being only two families (and probably only two genera) present throughout Beds I and II. Since most of the material is associated with living sites the selective factor of primate activity cannot be eliminated. In other words, the fish remains may only show which species the contemporary inhabitants were able to catch. *Clarias* often come into shallow water, and may even leave the water for short periods; during their seasonal spawning runs the fishes are densely concentrated in small streams and can easily be caught by hand. The smaller, more actively swimming *Tilapia*, although also found in shallow water, would be more difficult to catch unless traps or spears were used.

Thus, it is tempting to explain the relative abundance of the clariid fossils in terms of both hominid activity and the biology of the fishes. This explanation would be more satisfactory, however, if it could be shown that species from other families (and with different habits) were also present in the area. Material from sites not associated with hominid activities would also be of great value.

Considered in broad ecological terms, the fishes tell very little about conditions in the waters of Olduvai. Species of *Clarias* are reasonably tolerant of hydrological conditions that would be lethal for other species. This applies particularly to stagnant deoxygenated water. Less is known of their salinity tolerance, particularly to alkalinity.

The next section of the report compares alkalinity tests that have been carried out in the present East African lakes and rivers in relation to the fish populations and the degree of alkalinity that is tolerated. No *Clarias* are known in lakes with very high alkalinity such as Manyara and Hannington, although they occur at Manyara in the marginal reed swamps where fresh-water streams enter the lake. On the other hand, cichlids, especially some species of *Tilapia*, have a high alkalinity, salinity and temperature tolerance and exist in the highly alkaline lakes of Manyara and Magadi.

Dr Greenwood continues:

Extant species of *Clarias* and *Tilapia* are found in a wide variety of habitats, both lacustrine and fluviatile. Thus it is impossible to draw any conclusions about the type of water body existing during the time span of Beds I and II; it need not, as has been suggested (Leakey 1965), have 'contained a considerable body of water'. Hay (Leakey 1965) thinks that during the periods of Beds I and II the lake was 'alkaline and rather strongly saline for most of its duration'. The presence of cichlids and clariids would not necessarily contradict this conclusion provided that the upper limits of the alkalinity and salinity were within the ranges discussed above.

Site FLK North (upper Bed I) is of particular interest since it has yielded only the remains of Cichlidae. Sample sizes from this site are small, but by analogy with other sites, at least a few clariid remains would be expected. Clariids are some of the most ubiquitous fishes in present-day African fresh waters. Their absence, when cichlids are present, might indicate strongly saline (especially alkaline) conditions, as in Lake Magadi today. Since earlier and later fish-bearing deposits contain both clariids and cichlids, there does seem to be a possibility that the lake was more saline during the deposition of the FLK North bed than at other periods.

Any comparison of Beds I and II is complicated by the great disparity in sample sizes from the two deposits. The smaller samples from Bed II could account for the few cichlid remains available. On the other hand, we cannot overrule the possibility of different hydrological conditions during Bed II times. The most obvious change indicated by the presence of *Clarias* and the scarcity of cichlids is the development of serious deoxygenization, probably swamplike conditions.

REPTILES

Amphibians, Small Reptiles and Snakes

A variety of fossil amphibians, small reptiles and snakes has been found at Olduvai. Although his report is not yet complete, Dr J. C. Rage of the Institut de Paléontologie, Paris, has supplied me with some preliminary notes.

The collection includes the following: three genera of frogs, a toad, an agama lizard, a skink, a chameleon, two forms of python, a house snake, a sand snake, possibly a water snake, an egg-eater, a spitting cobra, a large viperine snake and probably a puff adder. The remains are from four sites in Bed I, from one in upper Bed II and one in Bed IV, where the skeleton of the python was found.

At DK in lower Bed I, no frogs, toads, lizards, chameleons or skinks have been recovered and the only reptiles other than crocodiles and turtles are a python, sand snake, spitting cobra and probably a puff adder. Three sites in middle and upper Bed I have mostly yielded the same species of amphibians and reptiles. My eldest son, Jonathan, who is a herpetologist, informs me that all the frogs (*Xenopus*, *Rana* and *Ptychadema*) are varieties now common in East Africa and that all are associated with permanent or semi-permanent water. (A species of *Ptychadema*, *superciliaris*, is found today at Olduvai, although the Olduvai River dries up seasonally.) The toad (*Bufo*) is also a widespread genus.

Chameleons have been found throughout Bed I and in upper Bed II; they resemble the living three-horned chameleon, *C. jacksoni*. In spite of the extensive excavations carried out in lower and middle Bed II none has been found at these levels. Present-day species require a bush or woodland habitat, rather than open plains, and their absence at certain horizons may be due to environmental factors. The writhing skink (*Riopa*), that was found throughout Bed I, is common nowadays from the coastal zone to the highlands, and generally frequents sandy soil.

Jonathan's notes on the habitat required by the living snakes of the species found as fossils at Olduvai are as follows:

Python (*Python sebae*)
This occurs in all sorts of habitats, but I would say has to be within reach of permanent water. (However, the one that attacked the dog near the Fifth Fault at Olduvai in 1960 must have been without water for very long stretches of time.)

House snake (*Boaedon*)
This species often lives near human habitation because its main food is small rodents. It can be found anywhere that small rodents occur and is common in most habitats, whether wet or dry.

Sand snake (*Psamophis*)
This snake is common in dry habitats such as Baringo, Northern Province, Tsavo etc., and at Olduvai itself.

?Water snake (*Grayia*)
The identification is somewhat doubtful, but if it is correct the presence of this snake indicates the proximity of permanent water. It is only found today near rivers or lakes and generally at altitudes of 4000 to 5000 feet or more.

Egg-eater (*Dasypeltis*)
This snake is common in most habitats and feeds exclusively on birds' eggs, such as those of weavers.

Spitting Cobra (*Naja nigricollis*)
This is also a common snake in almost all habitats except

true forest. It feeds largely on rats, frogs, etc., and can be found in both wet and dry areas; it does not need access to permanent water.

Puff Adder (*Bitis olduvaiensis*)
The present-day puff adder (*Bitis arietans*) can be found in almost every habitat, whereas the other two large vipers (*B. gabonica* and *B. nasicornis*) are only found in more or less forested areas and in fairly close association with permanent water. All feed mainly on small mammals and are terrestrial in their habits.

With the exception of the last species, a large viperine snake that is sufficiently distinct from the living vipers to merit separate specific rank (*B. olduvaiensis*), the fossil snakes stand close to those living in the Olduvai area today, where spitting cobras, sand snakes and egg-eaters are the most common varieties. No mambas are represented among the fossils. They exist in the area today, but are very rare; in fact I have seen only two examples during the last few years.

The one anomaly among the snakes is the water snake from FLK North, of doubtful identification; it clearly does not fit with the ecological conditions.

Crocodiles

This group of reptiles is being studied by Dr E. Tchernov of the Department of Palaeontology, the Hebrew University, Jerusalem. He has kindly provided me with information on which to base the following notes.

Pleistocene crocodile remains have been collected from three principal localities in East Africa: Olduvai, East Turkana in Kenya and the Omo Valley in southern Ethiopia.

The differences evident amongst the crocodile populations from the three areas indicate that these localities became cut off from one another in very early times.

The lack of contact in the aquatic fauna is understandable in the case of Olduvai, 800 kilometres south of the other two areas, but is difficult to explain in the case of East Turkana and the Omo Valley, both of which are within the Turkana basin.

The living crocodiles are divided into four families with separate geographical distribution. These are the crocodiles proper (Africa), gavials (Asia), tomistomids (Malaysia) and caymans, etc. (America). Both the gavials and tomistomids are characterized by exceedingly long and slender snouts that are specially adapted for catching and eating fish rather than mammals (during the Eocene they were, in fact, marine reptiles, but afterwards moved to inland waters). Members of both the other crocodile families have broader and shorter snouts, better adapted to catching and eating animals.

Among the fossil crocodiles from East Turkana and the Omo Valley are two species of *Euthecodon*, an extinct tomistomid. The two species are differentiated by the patterns of their nasal bones; and each species is confined to its own area, i.e. either East Turkana or the Omo Valley, proving that there can have been no interchange of these reptiles between the two localities in Lower Pleistocene times. The Nile crocodile – which lives in East Africa today – is found in both areas, as well as *C. catafractus*, a crocodile that today is confined to the Congo basin and Lake Tanganyika.

An extinct crocodile with a broad, squat muzzle is found at East Turkana, the Omo Valley and also at Olduvai (where it was first identified). This species sometimes reaches gigantic size and a skull from East Turkana measures one metre in length, with proportionate breadth. No living representative of this crocodile exists and it has been found as a fossil only in East Africa.

At Olduvai itself there are only two fossil crocodiles: *C. niloticus* and the newly identified broad-snouted, extinct species mentioned above, which is as yet unnamed. Neither *Euthecodon* nor *C. catafractus* is present, although Olduvai is geographically a great deal closer to the present habitat of *C. catafractus*, in southern Tanzania, than is the Turkana basin.

BIRDS

Dr Pierce Brodkorb, of the University of Florida, who is studying the fossil birds from Olduvai, has provided the following preliminary note and table.

Anthropological sites at Olduvai Gorge have yielded literally thousands of bones of birds. These represent groups of varied habits and ecological requirements, so that they furnish us with a good picture of the environments in which man underwent most of his evolution. They also provide us with several series of lineages in avian evolution.

Although this tremendous collection is still in a preliminary stage of study, it is possible to state that the fossil avifauna of Olduvai Gorge is among the largest heretofore known. The collection contains a minimum of thirty-three families (see table) and includes more than half the non-passerine families that occur today on the African continent. As the study progresses, other families will undoubtedly be identified, especially in the great order of Passeriformes. Olduvai Gorge is one of the few fossil localities in the world with more than fifty species of birds. The minimum number of species in the collection is fifty-seven, and this too will increase with further study.

Abundant remains of aquatic birds indicate that water was much more plentiful throughout the time of deposition of the earlier strata that form Beds I and II than is the case under the present semi-desert conditions. The water birds included swimmers and divers such as grebes, cormorants, pelicans and many ducks. Marine birds were represented by gulls, terns and skimmers. Waders were abundant and included flamingoes, herons, storks, rails, jacanas, plovers, sandpipers and stilts. The presence of flamingoes at several sites in both Bed I and Bed II indicates the proximity of brackish water.

Seed-eaters include francolins, quail and several species of doves. They demonstrate the presence of grassland.

Predatory birds and scavengers are scarce. The chief predators were owls, whose cast pellets were probably responsible for the numerous remains of small birds. Only an occasional hawk or vulture appears in the collection.

The bird remains from Olduvai will help us understand the rate of evolution, as most of them are of earliest Pleistocene age, a time that has not yielded many birds in other parts of the world. In some groups, particularly the grebes and cormorants, we will be able to trace lineages of species that occur in the modern avifauna. The indications are that most, perhaps all, of the birds from Bed I represent extinct species. In Bed II some of the species of Bed I have been replaced by another set of extinct species. Unfortunately, few birds were collected in the late Pleistocene beds, but they seem to indicate that the modern African avifauna became established then.

FAMILIES	VERNACULAR NAMES	GENERAL HABITAT OF LIVING FAMILIES	DK	MK	BED I			HWK	FC	BED II			
					FLK NN	FLK	FLK N			FLK	SHK	DC	BK
Strutionidae	Ostriches	Plains, semi-desert, open thorn bush	X										
Podicipedidae	Grebes	Aquatic, fresh-water and alkaline lakes, rivers			X	X							X
Phalacrocoracidae	Cormorants	Aquatic, widely distributed on inland waters			X	X		X					X
Pelecanidae	Pelicans	Aquatic, common on inland waters	X	X		X			X				
Phoenicopteridae	Flamingoes	Aquatic, brackish to saline water	X					X				X	X
Ardeidae	Herons, Egrets	Aquatic, swamps and marshes	X		X	X	X	X		X	X		
Ciconiidae	Storks	Aquatic and in flocks on plains			X	X	X						
Balaemicipitidae	Whale-headed stork	Aquatic, papyrus swamps				?	X						
Anatidae	Ducks and Geese	Aquatic, fresh and alkaline water			X	X	X				X		
Accipitridae	Hawks	Varied habitat			X	X	X						
Phasianidae	Francolin, Guinea fowl	Bush and open plains			X	X	X						
Turnicidae	Button Quail	Tall grass			X	X	X						
Rallidae	Crakes, Rails, Coots, Moorhens	Marshes	X		X	X	X						
Jacanidae	Lily Trotters	Aquatic, require floating vegetation			X		X						

Family	Common name	Habitat					
Charadriidae	Plovers	Lake shores and rivers, also open plains			X	X	
Scolopacidae	Snipe	Swamps, edges of lakes	X				
Recurvirostridae	Avocets, Stilts	Lake shores, saline and fresh-water				X	
Laridae	Gulls and Terns	Aquatic, inland waters and coast	X		X		
Rynchopidae	Skimmers	Aquatic, lake shores			X	X	
Columbidae	Doves and Pigeons	Varied habitats		X	X	X	
Cuculidae	Cuckoos	Varied habitats		X	X	X	
Psittacidae	Parrots and Love birds	Dry bush country, acacia and other forest				X	
Strigidae	Owls	Varied habitat			X	X	
Apodidae	Swifts	Varied habitat				X	
Coliidae	Mousebirds	Varied habitat				X	
Upupidae	Hoopoes	Dry bush and brachystegia woodland		X			
Capitonidae	Barbets	Savannah, acacia woodland					
Picidae	Woodpeckers	Varied habitat			X	X	
Hirundinidae	Swallows, Martins	Varied habitat			X	X	
Corvidae	Crows	Varied habitat			X		
Turdidae	Thrushes, Chats, Wheatears	Varied habitat			X		
Sylviidae	Warblers	Varied habitat				X	
Misc.	Perchers, Song birds	Varied habitat					
Passeriformes			X		X	X	X

MAMMALS

Insectivores: Elephant Shrews, Shrews and Hedgehogs

Professor P. M. Butler, lately of the Royal Holloway College, University of London, has studied the insectivores from Olduvai with the help of Mrs Marjorie Greenwood. Only the studies of the elephant shrews and the hedgehogs have been completed to date and Professor Butler has kindly sent me the following notes:

As far as ecological conditions are concerned, the elephant shrews have been the most informative so far. The commonest species is related to *Elephantulus (Nasilio) brachyrhynchus*, and especially to *E. fuscus*, a species from Malawi and Mozambique that has recently been distinguished specifically from *E. brachyrhyncus*. We have named the Olduvai form *E. fuscus leakeyi*. At the present day *E. brachyrhyncus* and *E. fuscus* are found in areas where the annual rainfall is 800–1600 millimetres. The present rainfall at Olduvai is below this and *E. brachyrhyncus* does not occur there, being replaced by *E. rufescens*. It is therefore inferred that during the time represented by the upper part of Bed I (i.e. FLK North) the rainfall was higher than at present.

Elephantulus is most common in the uppermost levels of FLK North. It is common, but much less common, in the middle levels, but only single specimens have been found in the lowest level at FLK North, at FLK, or FLK NN. It is suggested that this change reflects a progressive reduction of rainfall in Bed I times; at first the climate was too wet and the optimum conditions were reached by the top level at FLK North. This hypothesis is supported by the succession of species of Soricidae (shrews). The most common shrew in lower Bed I is an extinct species of *Sylvisorex* which is completely absent at FLK North. It is accompanied at one site by *Myosorex cf. robinsoni*, which becomes the commonest shrew at FLK North, level 5, and persists to the top of Bed I. A species of *Suncus* (another shrew) makes its first appearance (one specimen) at FLK and reaches its maximum at FLK North, in the upper levels, where it is by far the commonest shrew. We hope soon to gather information about the nearest living relatives of these shrews.

The hedgehog, *Erinaceous broomi*, is confined to FLK North where it reaches a maximum in level 4 (the middle level) and declines in the upper levels. It is an extinct species, not very closely allied to anything living today, though there is some resemblance to *E. albiventris*, the hedgehog now found in East Africa.

The insectivores of the upper part of Bed I represented at FLK North are very much like those found in the early Pleistocene cave deposits of the Transvaal (South Africa). There are indeed slight differences, but no more than one would expect to find in contemporary mammals living today in localities so far apart.

Species shared with South Africa are absent or very rare in lower Bed I. It looks as if the top of Bed I had a climate more like that of the Transvaal, but the lower part of Bed I was different, probably wetter. At Makapansgat the climate may have been drier than even the top of Bed I, as shown by the presence of *Macroscelides*, which today does not get above the 200 mm rainfall line.

Professor Butler adds that a study of the wear of the teeth of *Elephantulus* from Olduvai shows that there are many young individuals about six months old and another peak of older animals which could be a year older. A similar distribution was found in museum specimens of *E. brachyrhynchus* collected in the dry season (June to September) in East and Central Africa, but specimens collected during wet seasons do not show this distribution. Presumably the living sites at Olduvai would be flooded during the rains and the fossils found would represent mainly the dry part of the year.

Primates

My daughter-in-law, Dr Meave Leakey, has kindly supplied the information on which these notes are based.

Primate remains are rare in the Olduvai fauna, but among the fossils found at the *'Zinjanthropus'* site at FLK were remains of four bush babies or galagos. Professor Gaylord Simpson has studied these specimens and come to the conclusion that they were similar to, but not identical with, a living species of small bushbaby, *Galago senegalensis*, that today inhabits steppe and savannah country and has a very wide distribution.

Apart from galagos, the only fossil primate (other than hominids) that has been found in any quantity is a large extinct baboon known as *Theropithecus*, related to the modern gelada baboon that today is restricted to a very specialized habitat in the highlands of Ethiopia. *Theropithecus* has dental characters that are similar to the living baboon, *Papio*, but its teeth are higher-crowned and have a more complex cusp pattern. Most of the remains of *Theropithecus* from Olduvai consist of teeth and parts of skulls and mandibles, with a number of isolated limb bones. In 1962 Margaret Avery found an almost complete skeleton in upper Bed II, which has enabled the stature and body proportions of *Theropithecus* to be estimated. This specimen is now the type for the species known as *Th. oswaldi*.

The size and robustness of the limb bones indicate that this animal was very muscular, heavy and thick-set, and also of considerable bulk in comparison with the largest living baboons. The limb bones have been compared to those of a particularly large male *Papio* (*anubis*) and it has been demonstrated that both fore and hind limbs were substantially more robust, although similar in length. In the fossil, also, the fore limb was longer than the hind limb, while in living baboons the converse is found.

The mandible shows that the cheek teeth were larger than in the living baboons, whilst the incisors were smaller. In the skull the sagittal crest, which rises from the top of the skull as in male gorillas, is much more pronounced than in the living species; likewise the nuchal crest, to which the neck muscles are attached at the back of the skull. The muzzle was relatively short and high, but owing to the large cheek teeth it was longer than in the living baboons.

It seems likely that although the *Theropithecus* from Bed II may not have been of greater height than a large modern male baboon, it was probably twice as heavy.

In addition to the skeleton from upper Bed II there are enough specimens of *Theropithecus* from other sites to show that there was an evolutionary increase in size from Bed I to Bed IV. This is particularly well demonstrated by a female maxilla (upper jaw) from Bed IV in which the second molar is 5% longer than the second molar in the male specimen from Bed II. Since there is a high degree of sexual dimorphism in *Theropithecus*, as in living baboons, the male from Bed IV must have been considerably larger than the Bed II skeleton, and this, moreover, is much larger than the *Theropithecus* from Bed I.

There is a single skull from Bed I belonging to an animal with an exaggeratedly elongated muzzle. It resembles *Parapapio*, an extinct baboon which is common in South Africa in the australopithecine caves. A fragment of a small mandible which may belong to a magabey has also been found in upper Bed II.

Finally there is an unusual skull, again from Bed II, in which the cranial characters show affinities with the colobus monkeys, although the teeth are closer to the Cercopithecinae, the sub-family to which fossil and modern baboons belong.

Rodents

Dr J. J. Jaeger, of the University of Montpellier, France, has studied the rodents from lower, middle and upper Bed I. Nine different species of the family Muridae alone have been identified, of which eight are new.

It is of interest to note that the change from wet to drier conditions in Bed I and a return to wetter conditions in lower Bed II, indicated by other faunal evidence, is supported by the rodent population. The change does not seem to have been dramatic, since the majority of the rodent species present in middle Bed I is still present in the higher level, confirming the permanency of the lake and its associated vegetation. But the onset of new ecological conditions at the top of Bed I is indicated by the appearance of the gerbils and naked mole rats which favour dry savannah habitat.

The following notes deal with the habitats of the living genera of Muridae whose fossil counterparts are found in the fauna of Bed I:

Swamp Rat (*Oenomys*)

This is associated with humid conditions. It frequents long grass on the edge of swamps, high savannah country, secondary forest galleries and montane forest, but it is absent from dense primary forests. It is an agile climber and builds its nests in grass. It is not common in East Africa at present and is found only in Tanzania in the Mbisi Forest and on certain islands in Lake Victoria.

Tree Rat (*Grannomys*)

The living species of this arboreal genus generally lives in bush country and in galleries on the edges of forests. The genus has a wide distribution in the tropics.

Bush Rat (*Aethomys*)

Only the species close to the fossil from Olduvai (*Aethomys kaiseri*) can provide information concerning habitat and distribution. It is abundant on the Serengeti in fairly humid conditions, in dense patches of long grass in forest galleries. It has also been recorded in the swampy borders of riverine forests as well as in the open country of high savannah. It is abundant in the northern Serengeti, where the mean rainfall is 100 centimetres per year.

Broad-headed rat (*Zelotomys*)

This rare species has been caught on Mount Kilimanjaro at an altitude of 1750 metres, and also south of the Serengeti Park, in open grassland with scattered trees. Almost nothing is known of *Zelotomys woosmani*, whose present distribution seems to be limited to south-west Africa.

Swamp rat (*Pelomys*)

This species has been found on the Serengeti under relatively humid conditions with dense vegetation, at the edge of forest galleries that are dying out and also in grassland along streams and swamps. Cultivated areas are the usual habitat of this species.

Coucha rat (*Mastomys*)

In the Serengeti *Mastomys natalensis* seems to be particularly abundant in rocky outcrops and also in more humid grassland near water.

Grass mouse (*Arvicanthis*)

A. nilotocus appears to avoid dense vegetations and is less common in the humid areas of the northern Serengeti. Its preferred habitat is isolated patches of woodland on the open plains or else rocky inselbergs.

Tree rat (*Thalomys*)

T. paedulcus is an arboreal species whose presence seems to be linked with acacia thorns. This rodent shelters in holes in the thorn trees or lives in communal nests made of branches and thorns, sometimes at a height of several metres.

Thanks to the data supplied by a study of the living forms the following interpretations can be put forward.

1 The murid fauna of Bed I indicates a wetter environment than the present.

2 The murids characteristic of dense forest are poorly represented. Only *Oenomys* is present in middle and lower Bed I (FLK and FLK NN), but this genus is equally abundant in areas with humid herbaceous vegetation.

3 The new species *Aethomys lavocati*, *Zelotomys leakeyi*, *Mastomys minor* and *Pelomys dietrichi* seem to have represented marshy conditions, savannah with tall grass and papyrus swamps along the lake shore. *Aethomys lavocati* and *Zelotomys leakeyi* were the dominant species. It is not impossible that these ecological conditions were also the habitat of *Mastomys minor*.

4 The presence of a substantial proportion of arboreal rodents (*Thalomys*) that are linked with acacia thorn trees suggests that beyond the zone bordering the lake there was savannah with acacia woodlands.

5 The association of *Oenomys* and *Grannomys* in middle

Bed I (FLK and FLK NN) seems to indicate either a riverine gallery forest or dense bush; in either case this could have been a local phenomenon of little importance. These conditions seem to have disappeared at the time when the upper levels of Bed I were being laid down (FLK North).

6 Between middle and upper Bed I the changes in the Muridae are not so important as those evident in the other families or sub-families of rodents. This undoubtedly denotes the long duration of most of the riverine and lakeside conditions and also the very localized origins of the elements that constitute this fauna.

Carnivores

Carnivores are never common in the Olduvai fauna, but five families are represented among the fossils, most of which are from Beds I and II. A preliminary study by the late Dr R. F. Ewer of the material known in 1963 was published in volume I of the Olduvai monographs. Since her report was completed, many more specimens have come to light, particularly of the smaller forms such as mongooses. These have been studied by Mme G. Petter of the Musée National d'Histoire Naturelle, Paris. The following notes are based on both Dr Ewer's and Mme Petter's reports. The two ladies do not always agree on certain interpretations and in these cases I have given both points of view, at the risk of confusing readers.

Mme Petter states that she considers the fossil carnivores of Olduvai can be divided into three groups:

1 Ancient forms that survived into the upper part of the Lower Pleistocene, such as the machairodonts (sabretooth cats);

2 Large forms of existing groups that achieved a temporarily successful phase of evolution but did not survive beyond the early part of the Middle Pleistocene (among these are a jackal-like animal that attained the size of an African hunting dog, a large feline and a very large civet cat);

3 A group that included animals similar to present-day forms, in which the fossil species presumably filled the same ecological niches as the living animals of equivalent size.

There are also at least two species that appear to be ancestral to their living counterparts. These are *Prototocyon recki*, an extinct bat-eared fox, and *Crocuta crocuta ultra*, forerunner of the living spotted hyaena.

The sabre-tooth cats are the most interesting of the 'survival' animals. The remains from Olduvai are fragmentary and consist of part of a mandible and three limb bones from Bed I as well as a few teeth from Beds I and II. There is a well-preserved upper canine tooth from middle Bed II. This tooth and the fragmentary mandible belong to one of the smaller machairodonts, but the limb bones from Bed I, representing two individuals, are probably of *Megantereon* sp., one of the large species of sabre-tooth cats.

The three genera of carnivores that attained unusual size in Beds I and II times are the jackal (*Canis africanus*), the feline (*Panthera crassidens*) and the giant civet (*Pseudocivetta ingens*).

The large feline attributed to *Panthera crassidens* is an extinct form first described in South Africa, and its fragmentary remains have been found throughout the Olduvai sequence from Beds I to IV. It was intermediate in size between a lion and a leopard. A lower jaw that fitted neither lion nor leopard, found in upper Bed II, was provisionally attributed by Dr R. F. Ewer to this animal. Mme Petter, on the other hand, prefers to assign the specimen to a lion. It has also been compared to the lower jaw of the living tiger since it resembles tiger mandibles in the structure of the lower border. In lions, the lower border of the jaw is convex from front to back, so that if it is placed on a horizontal surface it can be rocked. In the tiger and in the fossil the lower border of the jaw is concave in the central part so that both ends rest squarely on a horizontal surface. Dr R. F. Ewer considered this character to be of sufficient importance to justify not assigning the mandible to a lion and suggests that it might possibly belong to the extinct feline *Panthera crassidens*. Mme Petter, however, states that a similar structure is occasionally seen in mandibles of lions, and prefers to assign the fossil to *Panthera leo* on the basis of its dentition. It is evident that further material is required before the status of this specimen and its relationship to *Panthera crassidens* can be determined; it is also possible that it should be classed with the machairodonts in the group of archaic survivals.

The giant civet cat is known only from Bed I and lower Bed II. The most complete specimen, consisting of half a sub-adult mandible with both deciduous and permanent teeth, was recovered from the same level as the type specimen of *Homo habilis*, at FLK NN. The size of this animal cannot be estimated with any certainty on the basis of the fragmentary remains that are available, but it may well have been nearly twice as large as the living civet, in which the maximum length of the mandible is from ten to eleven centimetres whilst in the fossil it is estimated to have been eighteen centimetres. The ecological position of this extinct civet is of interest and is discussed at some length by Mme Petter. She considers that the dentition indicates a largely omnivorous diet, in common with the living African civet cat which eats small mammals and reptiles, as well as insects, fruits and birds' eggs, when these are obtainable. On size alone, the extinct civet could be placed among the big predators such as leopards, cheetahs and hyaenas; but in order to fit within this group it would have needed to follow their way of living and have been capable of hunting fast-moving prey. There is no suggestion that it was adapted to rapid movement; moreover, its dentition would not have been suited to a purely carnivorous diet. Thus, it seems unlikely that this animal deviated appreciably from the general dietary pattern of the living civets, in spite of its great size. It is possible that during times of drought such a diet was insufficient for an animal of its size and this may have led to its extinction.

The hyaena *Crocuta c. ultra*, considered to be ancestral to the living spotted hyaena, was first described by Dr Ewer from the South African australopithecine caves in the Transvaal. The remains of this animal from Olduvai have so far been found only in Beds I and II. They include several mandibles as well as some limb bones. A considerable degree of morphological variation has been observed among these specimens; but it is not considered to be sufficient to warrant specific separation, particularly in the case of animals such as hyaenas, in view of their known adaptability to different ecological conditions and ways of living. In many respects the fossil hyaena resembles the extant form, but still retains a number of archaic traits.

Although the extinct genera and species briefly described above exhibit archaic characters that distinguish them from their living counterparts, the majority of the fossil carnivores from Olduvai correspond quite closely to the living forms. This is true of the jackal *Canis mesomelas latirostris* which is almost indistinguishable from the living black-backed jackal. There are also some remains of a leopard that appear to be very close to the living form. A few specimens have been attributed to *Hyaena hyaena*, the striped hyaena, but the material is too scanty to determine whether there was any close resemblance to the living animal.

Among the viverrids, the genus *Herpestes* (mongoose) branched out into a number of different species varying in size from that of the modern large white-tailed mongoose to the pigmy form. Three new species have been recognized by Mme Petter among the *Herpestes*, all of which are from Bed I. They are: *Herpestes* (*Garellela*) *primitivus*, *Herpestes* (*G*) *debilis* and *Mungos minutus*. There is possibly a marsh mongoose in middle Bed II, at MNK, but the identification is based on a single tooth and must be treated with caution. There is also part of a mandible, a femur and tibia resembling the living white-tailed mongoose.

Rare specimens attributed to the otter family are known from Beds I, II, III and IV. They appear to represent an animal intermediate between *Aonyx* and *Lutra*.

Mme Petter has attempted to compare and correlate the Olduvai carnivores with those from the South African australopithecine caves, but this is rendered extremely difficult on account of the undoubted difference in ecology between the two areas and the uncertain dating of the South African sites. Furthermore, only the large predators are known from South Africa, so that the extensive viverrid population of Olduvai is without parallel there. In both areas archaic forms such as machairodonts are found side by side with more evolved animals that were heading towards their extant counterparts. Certain genera are also common to both areas and appear to be represented by very similar animals. These include the ancestral hyaena *Crocuta c. ultra*, a leopard close to the living species and the large, extinct feline *Panthera crassidens.* Beyond such established facts it is doubtful whether the carnivora from the two areas can usefully be compared.

Proboscidians

The study of fossil elephants from East Africa made by Dr Vincent Maglio, formerly of Princeton University, has shown that the elephant underwent a period of diversification and expansion during the early Pliocene which gave rise to three major lineages in Africa: *Loxodonta*, which finally evolved into the present-day African elephant; *Elephas*, which once had a number of subsidiary branches, but is now represented only by the Indian elephant; and *Mammuthus*, whose last representative was the woolly mammoth. In *Loxodonta* the teeth are narrow; they are not so high-crowned as the teeth of other groups and have fewer ridges of enamel. The tusks also tend to be straighter. Representatives of *Loxodonta* are found during the Pleistocene in southern Europe, Asia and have also now been found at the Pliocene sites of Laetoli and Hadar in East Africa. *Elephas* has a short, deep skull, domed on top. The molar teeth are broader and higher than in *Loxodonta* and have close-set enamel ridges. It is to this group that the fossil elephants of Olduvai belong.

In the later representatives of *Mammuthus* the tusks are long and curved, even to the extent of crossing one another, in aged individuals. In this group the number of enamel plates in the molars varies greatly between different species. Fossil representatives of *Mammuthus* are found in Asia, America, Europe and Africa.

As in the case of the rhinoceroses, a multitude of different names has been given to the various evolutionary stages of the elephants, many of which have been based on the morphology of the teeth alone, since they are much more commonly preserved than skulls. The number of transverse enamel plates per tooth and the thickness of the enamel, taken in conjunction with the width/height index of the molars, are all considered essential criteria for assessing the taxonomic position of a fossil elephant; but it is clearly much to be preferred if these characters can be related to the features displayed by the skulls.

The elephants from Olduvai appear to have undergone a gradual evolutionary change like that seen in the rhinoceroses and hippopotami. Dr Maglio attributes all the known specimens to *Elephas recki*, which he divides into four evolutionary stages, based on the character of the molar teeth. Only stages 3 and 4, from below and above the Lemuta Member respectively, are recognized at Olduvai itself, but stages 1 and 2 have been identified at East Turkana and the Omo basin.

The skeleton of a *Deinotherium* found at one of the Olduvai butchery sites appears to belong to the species *D. bozasi*. The Olduvai specimen, however, is probably larger than any previously recorded. Instead of tusks in the upper jaw, *Deinotherium* had downward-curving tusks in the lower jaw. Although it was a proboscidean it is considered not to stand close to the true elephants. It existed during the Miocene and Pliocene in Europe and Asia and survived into the upper part of the Lower Pleistocene in Africa. Like many other mammals, its ancestral forms were considerably smaller than the Pleistocene species. At Olduvai it is found in Bed I and lower Bed II below the Lemuta Member, generally in deposits that indicate swampy conditions.

Equids

The very large collection of fossil Equidae has partly been studied by Dr D. A. Hooijer, of the Rijksmuseum van

Natuurlijke Historie, Leiden. He has published a paper on the three-toed *Hipparion*, in which he states that the Olduvai *Hipparion* is a fully-fledged '*Stylohipparion*' that does not differ dentally from *H. lybicum* of the Villafranchian (Lower Pleistocene of North Africa) or *H. steytleri* of South Africa.

These three-toed hipparions were originally adapted for walking on swampy ground, but by the time they had evolved into the Pleistocene form found at Olduvai the lateral toes seem to have become a residual feature. Furthermore, hoof prints found at the Pliocene site of Laetoli do not show any impressions of the lateral phalanges.

There is also a very large true horse (Equus) among the Olduvai fauna, which has been named *Equus oldowayensis*. A description of this group has not yet been published.

Rhinoceroses

Dr Hooijer has also studied the fossil rhinoceroses from Olduvai and has considered them in connection with the late Miocene rhinos from Fort Ternan in Kenya, Pliocene specimens from Laetoli and a few from the Omo basin in southern Ethiopia, of a similar age. The Olduvai rhinos can thus be studied against a background of the rhino population of East Africa extending over a very much longer period of time than is represented at Olduvai.

Dr Hooijer states that there are only two species of rhinoceros in the Pleistocene of East Africa, despite the fact that palaeontologists have described the fossils under a number of different names. The two species are ancestral to the two living forms, that is the white rhino (*Ceratotherium simum*) and the black rhino (*Diceros bicornis*). The two species probably became separated in the early Pliocene, when the white rhino branched off from the black rhino stock. The series of skulls that were found at Fort Ternan (about fourteen million years old) all belong to the black rhino lineage. They are quite small and the animal appears to have been a browser, like the present black rhino, and not a grazer, like the white variety.

In Pliocene and early Lower Pleistocene deposits, at Laetoli, in the Omo Valley and at Olduvai, below the Lemuta Member, the white rhino predominated. At Olduvai, in fact, there are no examples of the black rhino before the time of the Lemuta Member. According to Dr Hooijer the white rhino underwent a gradual evolutionary change during early and middle Pleistocene times, until it reached its present form. Such evolutionary changes can be detected with certainty only in the upper molar teeth, so that the number of specimens capable of yielding information is necessarily limited. However, there is sufficient material available to show that the earlier examples of the white rhino from Olduvai are very close to the primitive form from Laetoli. During Bed II times there was a tendency for the crowns of the teeth to become higher and also for an overall increase in the size of the animal. By Bed IV times the skull and dentition of the white rhino are almost indistinguishable from the present form, although the skull found in 1962, in Bed IV, is exceptionally large by present standards.

Although the black rhino does not occur at Olduvai as early as the white rhino, it is known in early Lower Pleistocene deposits in the Omo Valley and in the Pliocene at Laetoli. This early form is said to be very similar to the present-day black rhinoceros and to differ only in having larger and lower-crowned teeth.

Suids

Of all the groups of mammals that flourished during the later part of the Lower Pleistocene and the Middle Pleistocene and attained an unprecedented size the Suidae (pigs) must take pride of place.

There are three genera of Suidae in Africa at present, all of which have forebears in the Pleistocene. These are: the bush pig (*Potamochoerus*) which favours thick bush or forest habitat, the giant forest hog (*Hylochoerus*) which is a forest-dweller, and the warthog (*Phacochoerus*) which lives in open savannah country. A fourth genus, *Notochoerus*, flourished in the Pliocene but died out during the early Pleistocene.

Unfortunately, the fossil remains of Suidae from Olduvai are very fragmentary and only a small number of associated upper and lower dentitions is known. During the last few years, however, magnificent series of suid skulls have been collected from Kanapoi, East Turkana and the Omo Valley and have recently been published.

An outstanding example of a Middle Pleistocene suid was *Stylochoerus*. This animal was nearly as large as a small adult hippopotamus and had tusks in the upper jaw that measured one metre in length. This is a common suid in upper Bed II, particularly at site BK.

Remains of Suidae from Bed I and lower Bed II below the Lemuta Member do not show the increase in size that culminated in upper Bed II with *Stylochoerus*.

Hippopotami

The late Mrs S. C. Coryndon kindly supplied the following notes on the specimens from Olduvai:

In many parts of Africa today hippopotamus meat is a very popular item of diet, and the capture of a hippo provides meat for many people. As it is now, so it was in prehistoric times. The early hominids who lived in the area now known as Olduvai Gorge must also have relished hippo meat, as there is evidence on many of the hominid living sites that this animal was a common item of diet. Living near the ancient lakes, the early men were close to the home of the hippos, who presumably spent most of the daylight hours partially immersed in water, coming to the shore at dusk to graze. This was the time when the animal was most vulnerable to capture, and one can envisage groups of hominids lining up between the hippo and the sanctuary of the lake, while other members of the party set about the slaughter. After the meat was chopped and the bones smashed to extract marrow, the remains of the animal were left lying on the ground near the lake where many of them were subsequently preserved as fossils. Remains of fossil hippo have been found throughout the deposits of Olduvai Gorge from the lowest levels of Bed I, to the top of Bed IV. With one exception, these hippopotami belong to one species, *Hippopotamus gorgops Deitrich*. In the lower levels in Bed I this species is not unlike the familiar *Hippopotamus amphibius* of today; but even at that early stage ($1\frac{3}{4}$ million years ago) the characters that distinguish the species *H. gorgops* from all others were already apparent. In particular, the orbits (eye sockets) were higher than in the extant species, an indication of a truly amphibious habitat. As time went on, and the animals of Olduvai became more and more isolated from those in other parts of East Africa, certain groups of animals, and in particular the hippos, would evolve in their isolation and develop certain characters which were advantageous to them in the rather special conditions prevailing at that time. The ancient lakes fluctuated in size, and sometimes almost disappeared. They probably became more and more alkaline; and with the increasing brackishness, so the orbits of the hippos became higher, enabling them to remain in the water for long periods with only their eyes and the tips of their noses showing above the level of the lake. The fossil remains that have been found in the various deposits at Olduvai show clearly that the hippos of the lower levels were relatively unspecialized, with comparatively short faces and orbits only a little higher than in the living hippopotamus. As time went on, the remains from higher levels show that the animals evolved higher and higher orbits and longer and longer faces, until by the time Bed IV was laid down about 800,000 years ago *H. gorgops* had become what must have been a rather grotesque-looking animal with a long, rather flat face, huge protruding orbits and a massive lower jaw carrying immense tusks.

Although the large *H. gorgops* was the common hippopotamus of Olduvai Gorge throughout the history of the deposition of the sediments, there was one other very different hippo whose scanty remains have been found only in upper Bed II. This was a tiny animal in comparison with the large *H. gorgops* and, although we know him only from the partial remains of a hind leg and a lower jaw, it is clear that this was a very different animal. Instead of the huge tusks of the large hippo, this pigmy form had tiny little peg-like incisor teeth and small canine tusks. The hind leg was slender and the animal capable of running fairly fast; probably it behaved much more like a bush pig than the amphibious forms of hippopotamus. It could not compete for habitat with *H. gorgops* but was able to survive by living more on land where there was a fair amount of vegetation cover, coming to the water only to drink, as so many living bush and plains animals do.

Giraffes

The Giraffids are represented at Olduvai by *Giraffa jumae*, *G. stillei* and *Sivatherium*. Most of the remains are fragmentary and consist of incomplete mandibles, teeth and broken limb bones; but the greater part of a skeleton of *Giraffa jumae* was found in lower Bed II during 1959.

Giraffa jumae was first recognized as a distinct species by Louis and described in volume 1 of the Olduvai monographs. The specimen on which he based his diagnosis was a rather crushed skull that he found at Rawe, in Kenya, during 1934. Owing to the poor condition of the cranium, the distinctiveness of the species was based largely on characters in the mandible. In 1963, however, a complete cranium was found at Olduvai in middle Bed II at the Acheulean site EF-HR. The cranium was entirely on its own, totally devoid of any other parts of the skeleton, and must surely have been brought to the site by man. This cranium is also slightly crushed, but not to the extent of the Rawe specimen, so that the characters which distinguish it from the skulls of present-day giraffe are clearly evident. (It is even possible that the crushing of the top of the skull may have been caused by prolonged use as a seat.)

The cranium is approximately the same size as that of a full grown adult of the living species, but it differs substantially in having a much flatter frontal region or forehead, and also in the angle of the horns, which slope gently backwards almost in line with the forehead rather than rising steeply as in the modern giraffe. (In giraffes, the bony core of the horn, known as an ossicone, is covered with skin during life, whereas in bovids there is a covering of true horn or keratin, a nitrogenous compound.) *Giraffa jumae* also lacks any constriction between the outer rims of the orbits and the base of the horns, such as characterizes the living giraffes.

During 1970 parts of two skulls and a mandible of a very small giraffe were discovered at East Turkana, in Lower Pleistocene deposits. Although the Giraffidae from the Upper Miocene site of Fort Ternan, in Kenya, are of very small size, this discovery was wholly unexpected, since the existence of such a small giraffe during the Pleistocene had never been suspected. In the light of the new discoveries, Dr John Harris decided to re-examine the small giraffid teeth from Olduvai and came to the conclusion that they belong to a true pigmy giraffe and not to an okapi. An immature mandible from the *'Zinjanthropus'* level at Olduvai has been made the paratype of the species. Teeth have been found in Bed I and Bed II as well as upper Bed IV, so that it appears to have spanned the whole Olduvai sequence.

The short-necked and heavily-built 'antlered' giraffid, known as *Sivatherium olduvaiensis,* is never a particularly common fossil, but is present in nearly all levels throughout the Olduvai sequence. Teeth and parts of the massive knobbed ossicones are usually best preserved as fossils. To compensate for weight, the bones of the skull are filled with air cells, a process known as pneumatization. The bone itself, therefore, is relatively thin and fragile, and the skulls are rarely preserved. In spite of the numerous ossicones that have been found at Olduvai, there is only one rather incomplete skull in which their emplacement is preserved. This shows them to have risen almost vertically, with a backward sweep.

Bovids

The Bovidae, which include all the antelopes and gazelles, is the biggest group of large mammals in the Olduvai fauna. Their remains sometimes amount to as much as 80% of the identifiable faunal material on a living site, and the average figure for the twenty-one different sites or levels excavated in Beds I and II amounts to over 50%. This is made up of bones, teeth and horn cores belonging to numbers of different individuals, since it is very seldom that articulated or even partly articulated skeletons are preserved on living floors. At one site in Bed IV, however, Jonathan found a locality with the fossilized remains of a herd of antelopes. The bones and skulls were so tightly packed together that fifteen skulls and skeletons were found within a space of forty-three square metres. The bones had been cracked and broken prior to fossilization and had subsequently been cemented together by lime, so that they were often distorted; but three of the skulls are sufficiently well-preserved for them to be identified as a species of antelope resembling the present-day South African blesbok, which has been named *Damaliscus agelaeius*. It is evident that the animals must have died catastrophically, perhaps clustered round a waterhole during a drought, or else by being driven into a swamp by man. Although a few quartz flakes were found with the bones, there were not as many artefacts as at other sites where it is believed that the animals had been driven into swamps.

A large number of different types of Bovidae is represented at Olduvai. They range from some rare specimens belonging to a pigmy antelope to the giant buffalo-like *Pelorovis oldowayensis*, which had a horn span of two metres. For the most part, however, the remains on the living sites

belong to medium-size animals like the present-day hartebeest and wildebeest; but some of the extinct species were
considerably larger than their modern counterparts, particularly in middle Bed II.

The fossil Bovidae include ancestors of all the following living animals: eland, kudu, oryx, roan and sable antelopes, waterbuck, kob, reedbuck, hartebeest, topi, blesbok,
impala and gazelles. As well as those that have descendants
living today, there was a number of species and genera
that died out entirely and left no issue, particularly among
the Alcelaphini, the tribe that includes the hartebeest and
wildebeest. But the best known and most spectacular of
the extinct species was certainly *Pelorovis oldowayensis*, which
is mainly found in Bed II.

Dr and Mrs A. Gentry, of the British Museum of Natural
History, have kindly supplied me with some general notes:

Most of the Olduvai antelopes are from lineages ancestral
or closely related to living forms and a minority is from
extinct lineages. As might be expected, later Olduvai
antelopes are more like living species than are the earlier
ones. The Bed IV eland, for example, is closer to the
living eland than is the Bed I wildebeest to the living
wildebeest.

The most abundant fossils belong to the Alcelaphini,
the tribe which includes hartebeest and wildebeest. There
are few or no remains of antelopes characteristic of forests,
e.g. duikers, bongo, etc.

The living antelopes to which Olduvai antelopes are
ancestral are not invariably those still occurring in the
Serengeti region today. At present, various species of
gazelle (*Gazella*) are found in the northern part of Africa
and extend south as far as Tanzania. Entirely separated
from them is the closely related springbok (*Antidorcas*)
of South Africa. Yet at Olduvai a fossil species of springbok

is commoner than gazelles, and it is believed that the South African springbok may have originated in East Africa.

At times the Olduvai antelopes have been larger than their living relatives. This seems to apply more to the antelopes of middle and upper Bed II than of other levels. The kudu of that time would appear very striking, were we to see it alive, so too an extinct relative of the roan and sable antelopes with horns at least as large as the most exceptional of living specimens.

The composition of the antelope fauna at Olduvai has changed from time to time. For example, two extinct relatives of the waterbuck and lechwe occur in Beds I and lower II, although they are not common. Both then vanish, but one (*Kobus sigmoidalis*) reappears at the junction of Beds III and IV in a form closer to the living waterbuck. In the intervening parts of Bed II are found sparse remains of kobs, which are related to waterbuck, but not so closely tied to the immediate vicinity of water. Fauna changes like these are presumably linked with local conditions.

Over the period from Bed I to middle Bed II the bovid fauna changed quite substantially. The degree to which this change was sharply localized at the boundary between lower and middle Bed II is not yet clear, and there is no reason to envisage mass extinctions, grand immigrations or dramatic mutations.

The minority of extinct lineages of Olduvai antelopes includes most of the large and spectacular forms. The long-horned *Pelorovis oldowayensis* was on a lineage related to that of the living African buffalo. Its probable descendants are known from late Pleistocene sites (contemporary with the last Ice Ages of northern continents) in several parts of Africa from Algeria to the Cape, but all are now extinct. *Megalotragus* was related to wildebeest and hartebeest, but was larger than either. It is known from Beds I to IV at Olduvai and from several sites in South Africa. Its long legs must have given it body proportions closer to hartebeest than wildebeest. Perhaps the oddest antelope to have come out of Olduvai is the unique frontlet with horn core of *Thaleroceros radiciformis*, collected by the early German expedition, and the only Olduvai bovid to have survived the Second World War in Munich. It probably came from Bed IV and may have belonged to the waterbuck/reedbuck group of antelopes.

Some of the extinct antelopes of Olduvai as well as the relatives or ancestors of living species had more advanced teeth than living species. This suggests that previously existing antelopes might have been more narrowly adapted to particular ways of life. Perhaps one of the consequences of the Pleistocene extinctions of bovids is that the survivors have wider niches.

The causes of Pleistocene extinctions of mammals in many parts of the world, particularly the larger mammals, are still being debated. In connection with this, it is interesting that there is no evidence for the extinction of any antelope lineage within the time span of Olduvai Beds I to IV. *Pelorovis* and *Megalotragus*, for example, have disappeared in or since the late Pleistocene; other lineages either last until Bed IV or are known from sites likely to post-date Bed IV. Admittedly there are some unique occurrences at Olduvai, but these are evidence as much for origins as for extinctions.

CHAPTER EIGHT
In Conclusion

THE DISCOVERIES at Olduvai, Laetoli, East Turkana, the Hadar and the Omo Valley in Ethiopia have all added greatly to our knowledge of the early hominids, but so far, Olduvai has made the greatest contribution as regards their way of life.

As more evidence accumulates, it becomes increasingly clear that anthropologists have previously underestimated not only the age of the hominid fossils, but also the cultural level that had been reached by man during the Lower and Middle Pleistocene. There are still tantalizing gaps in our knowledge, but they are gradually being filled, mostly by adding together rather insignificant pieces of evidence.

East Africa has been claimed by some to be the 'cradle of mankind'; others postulate an Asiatic origin for the early hominids. The question has not been resolved, but it is certain that the conditions for preservation of early fossils in East Africa are unparalleled elsewhere. Active volcanoes depositing ash at relatively frequent intervals combined with fluctuating lakes in closed basins have preserved the remains of early man, his tools and the contemporary fauna in an unprecedented fashion. Such a wealth of evidence leads to the assumption that man originated in East Africa. But it must be borne in mind that in late Miocene times an ape-like creature, *Ramapithecus*, who is generally considered to have been in the direct line of human ancestry, was not confined to East Africa. His remains have been found in India, Pakistan, Hungary and Turkey as well as in Kenya. On a hypothetical basis, therefore, it is possible that any one of these areas could be the so-called 'cradle of mankind', given suitable conditions of preservation. The evidence available at present, however, points to East Africa as having the greatest potential for further research.

We have virtually no information concerning the way of life of *Australopithecus boisei*. His remains are far less numerous at Olduvai than those of *Homo habilis*. If such evidence ever comes to light, it is most likely to be at East Turkana, where both his cranial and post-cranial remains are unusually plentiful. For the present, it is possible only to put forward hypothetical interpretations based on the morphology of the physical remains that have been found.

The skull of *Australopithecus boisei* has been exhaustively studied by Phillip Tobias and is the subject of volume 2 of the Olduvai series. The limb bones and other post-cranial material from East Turkana and the Omo Valley, however, have not yet been studied in any detail.

As Louis pointed out in his first announcement of the discovery, a number of features in the skull of *Australopithecus boisei* are more human than any found in the living apes. The teeth are highly specialized with enormous molars and premolars, and very small canines and incisors. (The size of the grinding teeth gave rise to the term 'Nutcracker Man', which was adopted by the popular press.) These same dental characters had been noted in *Australopithecus robustus* in South Africa, but it was considered that they must be a late specialization and that earlier specimens of this lineage would prove to have a less specialized dentition. In fact, there does not appear to be any appreciable difference between the early and later specimens. Although there is some division of opinion, most workers regard this particular type of dentition as being adapted to a coarse, tough vegetarian diet rather than to meat-eating.

Evidence from the limb bones found at East Turkana, in the Omo Valley and the one fragment of femur from Olduvai indicates that *Australopithecus* had long arms compared to man. Following a study of the femur fragment from Olduvai, Dr M. H. Day has suggested that the stresses in the structure of the bone indicate that *Australopithecus boisei* may have been quadrupedal occasionally, an assumption supported by the length of the arm bones since discovered at East Turkana and in the Omo Valley. However, the position of the foramen magnum (the cavity in the base of the skull to which the spinal column is attached) indicates that the stance of the robust *Australopithecus* was more upright than any of the living apes: it is set considerably further forward, permitting the head to be carried in a more vertical position.

The potential capability of *Australopithecus boisei* for making tools is purely conjectural and largely a matter of individual opinion. There are, so far, no associated bones of the hand, such as are known of *Homo habilis* and the Hadar hominids, so that there is slender anatomical evidence as to the degree of manual dexterity.

Professor Dart has attributed the broken mammalian bones from the cave at Makapansgat to the activities of *Australopithecus africanus*, and for many years has been a fervent exponent of what he termed the 'Osteodontokeratic Culture'. He collected all the available bones, teeth and horn cores from the cave and classified them into various categories of alleged 'tools'. While it is evident that some of this material shows unquestionable traces of use, the fact that in many of the bones there is a pattern of fracture, often repeated in the same classes of bones, does not necessarily imply that the fractures were caused by human agency. There are inherent lines of weakness in all bones, along which they will break, irrespective of the immediate cause. Thus, a hominid smashing a limb bone to extract the marrow may end up with fragments similar to those caused by a carnivore breaking the bone for a like purpose; an apparent pattern in the types of fractures, therefore, does not necessarily imply hominid activity. For myself, I consider that tool-using and elementary tool-making in which only hands and teeth are brought into play were well within the scope of *Australopithecus boisei* and his South African counterpart. I do not think, however, that it is likely he had reached the mental status necessary for organized tool-making to a regular pattern, such as is present in the Oldowan industry. This involves a preconception of the tool it is desired to make and entails the use of one 'tool' to make another, i.e. a hammerstone or anvil by means of which the end-product is made. The position has been aptly summarized by Dr Kenneth Oakley in *Man the Toolmaker*:

> Possession of a great capacity for conceptual thought, in contrast to the mainly perceptual thinking of apes and other primates, is now generally regarded by comparative psychologists as distinctive of man. The systematic making of tools of varied types required not only for immediate but for future use, implies a marked capacity for conceptual thought.

Finally, *Australopithecus* had a brain size that was small relative to his estimated body size. *Australopithecus boisei* had a capacity in the region of 530 cubic centimetres, a figure that is below that of *Homo habilis*, although the body size of *Australopithecus* was undoubtedly greater.

I envisage *Australopithecus boisei* as a small-brained, robustly built, stocky creature, mostly bipedal, but perhaps occasionally resorting to all fours and squatting on his haunches when stationary or feeding. His diet was probably largely vegetarian, although he would almost certainly have eaten meat if it came his way and may have caught animals himself on occasion. How he lived is wholly problematical and any surmises must be based to some extent on the social structure of the living apes, allowing for a greater bias towards man.

Since 1960, when the first remains of *Homo habilis* were found, a great deal of additional material has come to light. One of the most important specimens is the nearly complete skull of OH24 from lower Bed I. All the parts of the skull that are considered to be essential criteria in assessing the taxonomic status of a fossil hominid are preserved, including the facial bones and the base of the skull, although it is crushed and somewhat distorted by earth pressure. The skull OH13 from the lower part of middle Bed II is also of great importance, since it demonstrates the continuation of the *Homo habilis* lineage into Bed II. Another skull, OH16, from the base of Bed II, although excessively damaged by Masai cattle, has a well-preserved dentition and enough of the vault, after reconstruction, to show that it should be included in the habiline group; however, some workers would place it in the bigger-brained group exemplified by '1470' from East Turkana. Lastly, a considerable number of loose teeth have been recovered, so that it is possible to determine the variation in size and morphology within the dentition of *Homo habilis*. Regrettably, no further post-cranial remains of real importance have been discovered since the tibia and fibula and the hand and foot bones were found in the early 1960s.

From all this material a provisional assessment can be made of some of the physical characters of *Homo habilis;* but it must be borne in mind that when the detailed study of the specimens has been completed by Phillip Tobias modification and revision may be necessary.

The two leg bones indicate that *Homo habilis* was both slenderly built and short in stature. It has been estimated that this individual may have been no more than 1.35 metres tall; but it is always possible that this was a female and that the males were both taller and more robustly built. The adult foot bones indicate that the foot was also small, but with a human arch: it may have been about fifteen centimetres long from big toe to heel.

Recent discoveries of fossilized hominid footprints in the Pliocene deposits at Laetoli, dated 3.6 million years ago, show that the Pliocene hominids were entirely upright and bipedal. Furthermore, the structure of their feet is indistinguishable from the feet of living peoples who habitually walk bare-footed. Trails of three individuals have been found in which the average length of the feet is fifteen, eighteen and twenty-two centimetres.

Before the discovery of the skull of OH24, a cranial capacity of 657 cubic centimetres had been calculated for *Homo habilis*, based on the reconstruction of the two parietal bones (believed to be of a male) found at FLK NN. Actual measurement of the brain case of OH24, by water displacement, gives a figure of 560 cubic centimetres. But this does not make allowance for the post mortem flattening of the vault of the skull, nor the crushing inwards of the base. If this damage is taken into account, the cranial capacity may have been not far short of 600 cubic centimetres, a reasonable volume in relation to the estimated body size. This is one of the most significant features in which *Homo habilis* differs from either *Australopithecus*; the cranial capacity of the undistorted skull SK5 ('Mrs Ples', from Sterkfontein), attributed to *Australopithecus africanus*, is no more than 480 cubic centimetres.

Another feature separating *Homo habilis* from the australo-pithecines is the form of the notches at the base of the skull into which the condyles of the mandible fit. These are known as the mandibular fossae; in *Homo habilis* they are deeply incised, as in man, while in the australopithecines they are wide and relatively shallow. Likewise, although the position of the foramen magnum is further forward than in the apes, it is still further forward in *Homo habilis*, making its position more human.

Knowledge of the mode of locomotion of the early hominids was formerly based on post-cranial material. Important evidence in this connection was provided by the Olduvai foot bones from Bed I. Some authorities deduced a free-striding gait similar to that of modern man, others postulated a semi-upright gait. The evidence from the hominid footprints found in 1978 at Laetoli leaves no doubt as to which interpretation is correct and that even in Pliocene times man's ancestors walked with a free-striding, fully upright, bipedal gait.

As regards manual dexterity: indirect evidence is provided by the small retouched tools of the Oldowan industry, since it is clear that such tools could only have been made and used by beings possessing a precision grip. The few hand bones from Bed I support the evidence of the tools, as do the earlier hand bones from deposits at the Afar, from which a nearly complete composite hand has been assembled.

The dentition of *Homo habilis* differs markedly from that of the robust *Australopithecus* in size and morphology of the anterior teeth and of the molar-premolar series. The size of the canines suggests a meat-eating diet, a fact that can also be deduced without hesitation from the debris of animal bones on the living floors.

The picture of *Homo habilis* that emerges from the cranial and post-cranial remains briefly described above is of a slenderly built, small and agile creature, habitually bipedal, with a human foot and gait, who carried his head as upright as we do. His brain was larger than that of any *Australopithecus* and of a fair size in comparison to his stature, although, of course, very much smaller than in *Homo erectus* or *sapiens*. We still have not found any remains that can be assigned to *Homo habilis* later than the skull OH13 from the lower part of middle Bed II.

The application of the term *Homo* to this group of fossil hominids has been criticized. However, the tool-making ability of *Homo habilis* is now even more firmly established than it was in 1962 when the fossils were first attributed to *Homo*. They may not fulfil all the requirements for the genus *Homo* that were laid down by anatomists in the past, but it is questionable whether these are fundamental criteria rather than traditional ideas formulated by zoologists and others prior to the evidence that has come to light in recent years. A statement made by the late Sir Wilfrid Le Gros Clark, one of the foremost British anatomists who was also greatly preoccupied with human evolution, is worth bearing in mind. He wrote: 'Probably the differentiation of man from the apes will ultimately have to rest on a functional rather than on an anatomical basis, the criterion of humanity being the ability to speak and to make tools.'

It should be mentioned that a few workers, including my son Richard, consider that the hominid remains from Olduvai attributed to *Homo habilis* should be subdivided into *Homo* and *Australopithecus africanus*. They would place the original parietals and the broken skull of OH16 with *Homo habilis* and assign the skulls OH13 and 24 to *Australopithecus africanus*. For myself, I consider that there is insufficient evidence to support this view and that such differences as exist can be attributed to sexual dimorphism.

As we have seen earlier, the best preserved living sites

are in Bed I. They have usually been buried rapidly by the lake sediments and consequently the remains are less disturbed than at the later sites when conditions were not as stable. The physical condition of the fossil bones, however, is not always as good as in Bed II or Bed IV, since they were often on clay palaeosols and became cracked and broken before fossilization, owing to the expansion and contraction of the clay under changing wet and dry conditions.

Of the various types of sites where artefacts and food debris have been found at Olduvai, only living and butchery sites have so far provided significant information concerning the habits of early man. The living floors have provided us with evidence that *Homo habilis* did not exist in foraging groups like the present apes, but had camp sites to which food was brought, where it was shared by the group, and where domestic activities were carried out. These sites are generally situated near water – suggesting, perhaps, that a satisfactory means of carrying water had not yet been devised. It is probable that shelters of some form were built. Leaving aside the stone circle at DK and the possible emplacement for a wind-break at FLK, there have been suggestions at other sites that the debris on the living floors is not just a random scatter, but that there was some factor affecting its distribution; perhaps some form of dwellings of which no trace remains.

It has not been possible to detect any distinct grouping of different types of artefacts in particular areas of the living floors, such as occur at later palaeolithic sites – particularly in caves – where, for instance, an area with a preponderance of scrapers suggests that skins may have been worked on that particular spot. The central part of the living floor at FLK, however, presents a very different picture to the marginal zone. As we have seen, an area of about five metres in diameter inside the suggested wind-break was thickly strewn with small tools and flakes as well as large numbers of small bone fragments. The marginal areas, in contrast, contained larger bones and artefacts, as well as numbers of cobbles or manuports. Such a distribution of remains suggests that the central debris-strewn area was the focus of domestic activity; that it was protected from the prevailing wind by a form of wind-break, and that bones or other objects no longer required were thrown out over the fence.

The numbers of individuals who occupied these sites cannot be estimated, but, judged on conditions among the Bushmen, who probably provide the closest parallel among present-day hunter-gatherers, the bands of early man are unlikely to have been very large. This is a matter of economy, since when there is neither stock nor agriculture, it becomes impossible to obtain adequate food supplies for a large community in one area for any length of time. The Bushmen habitually live in groups of about twenty to thirty individuals, counting women and children, but band together into groups 100 strong on the occasion of special hunting expeditions. They have undoubtedly evolved a social structure best adapted to their hunting and gathering existence under particularly harsh conditions. It may well not be far removed from that of *Homo habilis*, whose needs were fundamentally the same. Given that the living sites were probably not occupied by large groups, the amount of bone debris that they contain is surprisingly abundant when compared to present-day abandoned village sites in Africa, in areas where hyaenas and other scavengers are active. Accurate estimates of the numbers of individual animals represented on the living sites have not yet been made, but it seems possible that the figures may not be very high in relation to the quantity of bones. If this is the case, perhaps the scavengers were less common or less hungry in Bed I times than they are now. It is possible that *Homo habilis* had favourite camping grounds to which he returned repeatedly, so that the bone debris accumulated over a period of time; but if this were the case, differential weathering of the bone fragments might be expected, a feature that has not been observed.

It is interesting to note that bones or teeth belonging to more than one hominid have been found at several sites. At FLK, there was not only the skull of *Australopithecus boisei*, but also teeth and skull fragments belonging to two juvenile individuals of *Homo habilis*. At FLK NN, there were parts of two adults and a juvenile of *Homo habilis*, as well as a broken premolar probably belonging to *Australopithecus*. The circumstances that gave rise to these multiple and apparently contemporary remains are difficult to interpret. Some of the bones have been chewed by scavengers and it is likely that the missing parts of the bodies were totally destroyed by them. *Homo habilis* appears to have left his dead lying on the camp floors and not attempted to dispose of them elsewhere. It might be expected that the presence of one dead body might have driven others in the group to move elsewhere. Thus, the possibility must be considered that violence or illness may have been responsible for killing a number of individuals simultaneously at one camp site, or within a short time of one another.

The number of animal bones on the living sites demonstrates that *Homo habilis* not only hunted, but did so successfully. A preliminary assessment of the material does not indicate that either very old or very young animals predominate. Both are represented but are no more common than mature adults, who presumably were not at any physical disadvantage when they were hunted and killed.

There is no direct evidence as to what methods *Homo habilis* may have used for hunting, other than the skulls of three antelopes from FLK North, which were evidently clubbed to death. Wooden spears were almost certainly used, perhaps also sharply pointed horns, and from the top of Bed I onwards there are stone balls which were perhaps used as missiles in the form of bolas. This suggested use is purely conjectural, but appears to be the most satisfactory explanation that has yet been put forward. Many of the spheroids are made with infinite care, commonly of gneiss or quartzite. Both these rocks were also particularly favoured for anvils, presumably because they are more resistant to blows than lava, a quality that would have recommended them for missiles.

In Bed I times the topography of Olduvai seems to have consisted of open plains surrounding the lake. It is unlikely, therefore, that herds of game could have been driven over cliffs, a method of hunting that came to be used in Europe in Acheulean and later times. An alternative method, which does seem to have been practised, was to drive the animals into swamps, particularly the heavily-built animals which would have difficulty in extricating themselves. As we have seen, an elephant, a *Deinotherium* and a herd of *Pelorovis* have all been found under conditions indicating that they died as a result of having become engulfed in mud. The occurrence of artefacts with these remains is clear evidence that man obtained meat from the carcasses; and it is quite possible that he was also responsible for driving the animals to their deaths.

The numbers of different groups of animals represented among the debris on the living floors vary to some extent from site to site, but antelopes are invariably the most common. They are usually of medium size, neither as large as an eland nor as small as a duiker. A few gazelles also occur, but they are not common. Equidae are also well represented. Man was hunting both the three-toed horse *Stylohipparion* and the big *Equus oldowayensis*. Remains of Suidae occur in about the same proportions and at some sites bones and teeth of suckling pigs are particularly common. Bones of the larger animals such as giraffe, *Sivatherium*, hippopotamus and rhinoceros are also found on the living sites, but the number of individuals represented is small.

The only clues that we have concerning the diet of *Homo habilis* are the remains that have become fossilized on the living floors. Roots, berries, nuts, insects, grubs and many other things were certainly eaten, but of these we have no trace. In Bed I times a variety of different creatures seems to have been eaten, as well as the larger mammals. Both catfish and *Tilapia* occur at nearly all the living sites and were particularly common at FLK NN, although turtles outnumbered every other group at this site. There were also vertebrae of a python and teeth of a viperine snake, as well as bones of rodents, frogs, toads and a few shrews. We have seen that the abundant remains of small mammals, birds, reptiles, etc. that were found in the upper part of Bed I at FLK North, were probably contained in owl pellets, but that a proportion of these creatures may also have been eaten by man, since their crushed bones were found in small piles, suggestive of human faeces.

Broken ostrich eggshells occur at most sites in Bed I, but are not so plentiful as in Bed II. Molluscs are rare, except for the site of skull OH13, where pieces of shell belonging to a large land snail (probably *Achatina* sp.) were abundant. Bony plates of Urocyclid slugs are common at DK and at some other sites, but since all these sites were near the lake shore it is impossible to determine whether the slugs formed an article of diet or died in their natural habitat.

The position concerning the hominid population of Bed II and its material culture is still obscure. As we have seen, *Australopithecus boisei* continued to exist even in the higher levels of Bed II. *Homo erectus* also occurs for the first time at approximately the same horizon, while the most recent

known *Homo habilis* was in the lower part of middle Bed II.
We do not know what happened to *Homo habilis*. Did he die
out, move elsewhere, or evolve into *Homo erectus*?

Since we have considered *Australopithecus boisei* in Bed I
to be an unlikely tool-maker, we can probably also count
him out of the picture for Bed II. It is possible, however,
that he may have evolved to some extent during the long
period of time represented by Bed II, and it is not incon-
ceivable that at this stage he was more capable of making
tools than his earlier antecedents.

The earliest and most informative specimen of *Homo
erectus* is the massive skull-cap (OH9) from upper Bed II. It
has a large cranial capacity, estimated at 1000 cubic centimetres; but this must be related to the body size of the
individual, which was probably considerable, judging by the
femur shaft and part of the pelvic girdle found in Bed IV
(OH28) also attributed to *Homo erectus*. In contrast to this
skull is the small skull OH12, also from Bed IV, which is
probably female and has an estimated cranial capacity of
700 cubic centimetres. Comparison with the skulls of *Homo
erectus* from China and the Far East shows that the skull
OH9 falls near the mean cranial capacity for the Chinese
series, but that OH12 is considerably smaller than any of
these and can be matched only approximately by the lowest
figure for the Far Eastern series, which is 750 cubic centimetres.

Apart from the two bones of OH28, the ulna from upper
Bed II and possibly the femur shaft from JK, no post-
cranial remains of *Homo erectus* have been found at Olduvai.
Virtually no information is available as to his physical
characteristics, other than the fact that OH9 had particularly
massive brow ridges and that in both this individual and
the small-brained OH12 the walls of the skull were exceedingly thick.

Much less is known about the living conditions and hunting ability of *Homo erectus* than of *Homo habilis*. This is due, as we have seen, to the unsatisfactory conditions under which debris from the living sites is found, i.e. in stream and river channels. Our knowledge is restricted to a bare list of tool types and of the animals represented among the faunal remains, that are, moreover, generally very fragmentary and do not yield much information. It can be stated, however, that remains of hippos are found at nearly every site, as well as catfish bones and crocodile teeth. *Tilapia*, which are not uncommon in Bed I, seldom occur. Since these fish have a much higher tolerance for alkaline water than catfish, the inference is that the aquatic fauna of Bed IV is more likely to have lived in fresh-water rivers than in any alkaline lake. Equid remains, particularly of *Stylohipparion*, the three-toed horse, are also abundant, but Suidae, which are so numerous in Bed II, are far less common.

Since no undisturbed living sites of *Homo erectus* have been found, their situation and extent are not known, but it is certain that they are closely linked with the streams and rivers; whether they were actually in the stream beds, on sand bars, or along the banks of rivers cannot be stated at present.

One outstanding question that remains unanswered concerns the coexistence of the Developed Oldowan and Acheulean. For what reason did these two traditions in toolmaking remain distinct over such a long period of time when they were within the same area and contemporaneous in the geological sense? Although a variety of explanations has been put forward, there is still no evidence to indicate which may be correct.

The years of fieldwork at Olduvai, briefly described in this book, have provided a great deal of information concerning early man. There is certainly no other site in the world that could have provided so much, and I consider myself greatly privileged to have undertaken the work.

A general outline of the hominid population, their way of life, stone industries and contemporary fauna has been revealed. This information is now firmly linked with the geological history of the Olduvai basin, but further studies are still required in certain parts of the sequence, particularly in middle and upper Bed II where the relationship of *Homo habilis* to *Homo erectus* is not known.

RECOMMENDED READING

Clark, J. Desmond, *The Prehistory of Africa*, Praeger Publishers, New York, 1970.

Cox, Allan, *Plate Tectonics and Geomagnetic Reversals*, W. H. Freeman, San Francisco, 1973.

Day, M. H., *Guide to Fossil Man*, Cassell, London, 1977.

Hay, R. L., *Geology of the Olduvai Gorge*, University of California Press, Berkeley, 1976.

Leakey, L. S. B., Olduvai Gorge, vol. 1, *A Preliminary Report on the Geology and Fauna*, C.U.P., 1967.

Leakey, M. D., Olduvai Gorge, vol. 3, *Excavations in Beds I and II*, C.U.P., 1971.

Leakey, Richard and Lewin, Roger, *Origins*, E. P. Dutton, New York, 1977.

Oakley, K. P., *Man the Toolmaker*, Brit. Mus. Nat. Hist., London, 1972.

Tobias, P. V., Olduvai Gorge, vol. 2, *The Cranium and Maxillary Dentition of Australopithecus (Zinjanthropus) boisei*, C.U.P., 1967.

Waechter, John, *Man before History*, Phaidon Press, Oxford, 1976.

Wood, Bernard, *The Evolution of Early Man*, Peter Lowe, London, 1976.

INDEX